G. SCHIRMER'S COLLECTION OF OPERA LIBRETTOS

COSÌ FAN TUTTE

Opera in Two Acts

Music by

W. A. Mozart

Libretto by
LORENZO DA PONTE

English Version by
RUTH and THOMAS MARTIN

Ed. 2031

G. SCHIRMER, *Inc.*

DISTRIBUTED BY

Important Notice

Performances of this opera must be licensed by the publisher.

All rights of any kind with respect to this opera and any parts thereof, including but not limited to stage, radio, television, motion picture, mechanical reproduction, translation, printing, and selling are strictly reserved.

License to perform this work, in whole or in part, whether with instrumental or keyboard accompaniment, must be secured in writing from the Publisher. Terms will be quoted upon request.

Copying of either separate parts or the whole of this work, by hand or by any other process, is unlawful and punishable under the provisions of the U.S.A. Copyright Act.

The use of any copies, including arrangements and orchestrations, other than those issued by the Publisher, is forbidden.

All inquiries should be directed to the Publisher:

G. Schirmer Rental Department
5 Bellvale Road
Chester, NY 10918
(914) 469-2271

Copyright © 1951 (Renewed) by G. Schirmer, Inc. (ASCAP) New York, NY
International Copyright Secured. All Rights Reserved.
**Warning: Unauthorized reproduction of this publication is
prohibited by Federal law and subject to criminal prosecution.**

COSÌ FAN TUTTE

Towards the end of 1789—two years before his death—Mozart was, as usual during this period of his career, in dire financial straits. On December 29 he wrote to his friend and fellow-Mason, Michael Puchberg: "According to the present arrangement I am to receive from the management next month 200 ducats for my opera. If you can and will lend me 400 gulden until then, you will be rescuing your friend from the greatest embarrassment . . ."

The opera in question was *Così fan tutte, osia la scuola degli amanti* (Women Are Like That, or The School for Lovers). Mozart had been since 1787 official composer to the Imperial Court at Vienna, at a salary of 800 gulden a year, but had been given little to do besides writing dances. A successful revival of *The Marriage of Figaro* in Vienna in 1789 (it was given twelve times from August to November), however, had impressed the music-loving Emperor Joseph II, and Mozart was commissioned to write a new opera. He set to work immediately and completed the music in January 1790.

While the libretto for *Figaro* was derived from a play by Beaumarchais and that for *Don Giovanni* from an opera by Bertati and Gazzaniga and other sources, the plot of *Così fan tutte* seems to have been invented by da Ponte.

Così fan tutte was performed for the first time on January 26, 1790, at the Burgtheater in Vienna.

The opera seems to have been fairly successful at first. Even Count von Zinzendorf, who had found *Figaro* a bore, thought "Mozart's music charming and the subject very amusing." After five performances the theater was closed for two months because of the death of Joseph II (February 20). When it was reopened, *Così fan tutte* was given five times more and then was dropped. But the following year it was performed in German at Frankfurt and Mainz and in Italian at Prague, Leipzig, and Dresden; and after Mozart's death it spread beyond Central Europe. Strangely enough, the first New York performance does not seem to have taken place until 1922.

Mozart lavished on this work some of his most delightful music, his most exquisite craftsmanship. If some of the arias are not perhaps as telling as the best in his other mature operas, they are outnumbered by the ensembles, which are wonderfully varied in style and construction. The orchestration is Mozart at his most sparkling—in other words, the finest to be found in 18th-century music. Occasionally a mock-serious piece, aping the style of the lamenting or heroic aria of the *opera seria*, underscores the gentle irony of the work. The sly humor extends even into the Overture, which, unlike that to *Figaro*, employs several themes from the opera. A subtle touch is the appearance here, as a tailpiece to one of the themes, of a jolly figure sung by Basilio in *Figaro* (Act I, No. 7) to the words *così fan tutte le belle*. It is difficult to see why *Così fan tutte* has not always been accepted, especially in our times, for what it is—a musical lark that is one of the gems of *opera buffa*.

N.B.

THE STORY

ACT I.

Don Alfonso, a cynical old philosopher, declares to his young friends Ferrando and Guglielmo that no women can be trusted, including their respective fiancées, the sisters Dorabella and Fiordiligi. Enraged at this slur, they accept his offer to wager 100 sovereigns that he can prove his point in twenty-four hours if they will agree to follow his instructions unquestioningly. Don Alfonso then announces to the two sisters that their sweethearts have been ordered off to the wars. There is a touching scene of farewell and the two officers ostensibly sail off, to the cheers of the villagers. Despina, maid to the sisters, finds them prostrated by their loss and pooh-poohs their lamentations, saying that one man is pretty much like another. To further his scheme Don Alfonso enlists Despina's aid and introduces to her two young and wealthy "Albanians" who are enamored of her mistresses. She does not recognize Ferrando and Guglielmo in their disguise and supports their suit. Fiordiligi and Dorabella are outraged at this intrusion upon their sorrow and angrily order the two foreigners to leave. When the young men pretend to take poison in their despair, the sisters relent somewhat. Despina appears in the disguise of a doctor and revives the "Albanians" by means of a huge magnet. They renew their ardent attack on the young ladies' affections but are again repulsed.

ACT II.

After Despina derides their constancy, the sisters, especially Dorabella, weaken and decide a flirtation will do no harm. Dorabella choose Guglielmo and Fiordiligi Ferrando. As the couples stroll in the garden Guglielmo wins Dorabella's love and gives her a golden locket in return for a picture of Ferrando. Fiordiligi, however, refuses to yield to Ferrando and decides to disguise herself as a man and join her betrothed at the front. But when Ferrando threatens to slay himself, she too gives in. Both Guglielmo and Ferrando are now utterly cast down by the clear evidence of their sweetheart's fickleness; but the triumphant Don Alfonso promises them that he will fix everything. He arranges a ceremony in which Ferrando is to marry Fiordiligi and her sister Guglielmo. In the midst of the ceremony, which is conducted by Despina in the guise of a notary, the military music to which the two officers marched off to war is heard again and it is announced that they have returned. In the confusion Ferando and Guglielmo leave the stage and come back without their disguises, explaining that they had received royal permission to return to the arms of their loved ones. The officers pretend to fly into a rage when they find the marriage contract, the sisters blame Don Alfonso and Despina for leading them astray, their lovers reveal that they were the "Albanians," Guglielmo returns Ferrando's picture to Dorabella and gets his locket back, the sisters are properly chastened, and all ends happily.

CAST OF CHARACTERS

FIORDILIGI . . . . Soprano

DORABELLA . . . . Mezzo-Soprano

GUGLIELMO, officer, betrothed to Fiordiligi . . . . Tenor

FERRANDO, officer, betrothed to Dorabella . . . . Baritone

DESPINA, chambermaid to Fiordiligi and Dorabella . . . . Soprano

DON ALFONSO, an old philosopher . . . . Bass-Baritone

Soldiers, Servants, Sailors, Wedding-Guests, Townspeople

PLACE: Naples

TIME: 19th century

SYNOPSIS OF SCENES

COSÌ FAN TUTTE

ATTO PRIMO

SCENA I

No. 1. TERZETTO

FERRANDO

La mia Dorabella
capace non è,
fedel quanto bella
il cielo la fè,

GUGLIELMO

La mia Fiordiligi
tradirmi non sa,
uguale in lei credo
costanza e beltà,

DON ALFONSO

Ho i crini già grigi,
ex cathedra parlo,
ma tali litigi
finiscano quà.

FERRANDO, GUGLIELMO

No, detto ci avete
che infide esser ponno,
provar cel' dovete,
se avete onestà.

DON ALFONSO

Tai prove lasciamo.

FERRANDO, GUGLIELMO

No, no le vogliamo:
o fuori la spada,
rompiam l'amistà.

DON ALFONSO

O pazzo desire!
cercar de scoprire
quel mal che trovato
meschini ci fa.

FERRANDO, GUGLIELMO

Sul vivo mi tocca,
chi lascia di bocca
sortire un accento
che torto le fa.

RECITATIVO

GUGLIELMO

Fuor la spada! scegliete qual di noi
più vi piace.

DON ALFONSO

Io son uomo di pace, e duelli non fo,
se non a mensa.

FERRANDO

O battervi, o dir subito, perchè d'in-
fedeltà le nostre amanti sospettate
capaci.

DON ALFONSO

Cara semplicità, quanto mi piaci!

FERRANDO

Cessate di scherzar, o giuro al cielo—

DON ALFONSO

Ed io, giuro alla terra, non scherzo,
amici miei: solo saper vorrei che
razza d'animali son queste vostre
belle, se han come tutti noi carne,
ossa, e pelle, se mangian come noi,
se veston gonne, alfin, se dee, se
donne son.

FERRANDO, GUGLIELMO

Son donne: ma son tali, son tali—

DON ALFONSO

E in donne pretendete di trovar fedeltà? Quanto mi piaci mai, semplicità!

No. 2 TERZETTO

DON ALFONSO

È la fede delle femmine
come l'araba Fenice,
che vi sia, ciascun lo dice,
dove sia,
nessun lo sa.

FERRANDO

La fenice è Dorabella.

GUGLIELMO

La fenice è Fiordiligi.

COSÌ FAN TUTTE

ACT ONE

SCENE I

No. 1. Terzet

FERRANDO

To doubt Dorabella is simply absurd,
Completely absurd!
She'll always be faithful and true to
her word!

GUGLIELMO

To doubt Fiordiligi would no more be
right,
Would no more be right,
Than trying to tell you the sun shines
at night!

DON ALFONSO

I'm well over sixty, I speak from ex-
perience,
But since you won't heed the advice of
a friend,
At least let us bring this dispute to an
end.

FERRANDO, GUGLIELMO

With no shred of proof you declared
them unfaithful.
An insult like that we could never
ignore.

DON ALFONSO

Don't ask me to prove it.

FERRANDO, GUGLIELMO

(putting their hands on their swords)
That's just what we ask you,
We want satisfaction,
Or else choose your weapon to settle
the score.

DON ALFONSO

You both must be crazy!
I only was trying to save you some
trouble,
And warn you of what is in store.

FERRANDO, GUGLIELMO

I can't take it lightly!
You slander unrightly
The highminded woman I worship,
Admire, and adore.
My honor is slighted,
Our friendship is blighted,
You wounded my pride to the core!

RECITATIVE

GUGLIELMO

Choose your weapon! You'll render us
complete satisfaction.

DON ALFONSO
(calmly)

I'm a peace-loving bachelor, and get
my satisfaction when I'm dining.

FERRANDO

Either fight with me or apologize for
casting all those slurs upon our
sweethearts and their good reputa-
tion.

DON ALFONSO

How can you be so blind! You make
me laugh!

FERRANDO

This joke has gone too far! I will not
stand for it!

DON ALFONSO

My friends, I can assure you, I spoke
in bitter earnest. May I ask one
question: what strange, uncommon
species do your lady-loves belong to?
Would you say they are goddesses,
boneless and bloodless, or do they eat
and drink like us poor mortals? Are
they angels or are they women?

FERRANDO, GUGLIELMO

They're women—but what women!

DON ALFONSO

They're women, and faithful? That you
really believe?
Are you so inexperienced, or just naive?

No. 2. Terzet

DON ALFONSO

Woman's famous faith and constancy
Is a myth and fabrication,
Though it makes good conversation,
Who can prove it?
Name me one name!

FERRANDO

I have proof in Dorabella!

GUGLIELMO

I have proof in Fiordiligi!

FERRANDO

Dorabella,

GUGLIELMO

Fiordiligi,

FERRANDO

la fenice è Dorabella.

GUGLIELMO

la fenice è Fiordiligi.

DON ALFONSO

Non è questa, non è quella,
non fu mai, non vi sarà.
E la fede delle femmine
come l'araba fenice!

FERRANDO, GUGLIELMO

La fenice è {Dorabella, Dorabella}
         {Fiordiligi, Fiordiligi}
è la fenice.

DON ALFONSO

Che vi sia, ciascun lo dice.

FERRANDO

Dorabella,

GUGLIELMO

Fiordiligi,

DON ALFONSO

Dove sia,

GUGLIELMO

Fiordiligi,

DON ALFONSO

Dove sia,

FERRANDO

Dorabella,

DON ALFONSO

Nessun lo sa,

FERRANDO

Dorabella,

GUGLIELMO

Fiordiligi.

DON ALFONSO

Nessun lo sa.

RECITATIVO

FERRANDO

Scioccherie di Poeti!

GUGLIELMO

Scempiaggini di vecchi!

DON ALFONSO

Or bene; udite, ma senza andar in
  collera: qual prova avete voi, che
  ognor costanti vi sien le vostre amanti; chi vi fè sicurtà, che invariabili
  sono i lor cori?

FERRANDO

Lunga esperienza—

GUGLIELMO

Nobil educazion—

FERRANDO

Pensar sublime—

GUGLIELMO

Analogia d'umor—

FERRANDO

Disinteresse—

GUGLIELMO

Immutabil carattere—

FERRANDO

Promesse—

GUGLIELMO

Proteste—

FERRANDO

Giuramenti—

DON ALFONSO

Pianti, sospir, carezze, svenimenti.
  Lasciatemi un po' ridere——

FERRANDO

Cospetto! finite di deriderci?

DON ALFONSO

Pian piano: e se toccar con mano oggi
  vi fo che come l'altre sono?

GUGLIELMO

Non si può dar!

FERRANDO

Dorabella!

GUGLIELMO

Fiordiligi!

FERRANDO, GUGLIELMO

No one else but {Dorabella!
                {Fiordiligi!

DON ALFONSO

Fiddle-faddle, fiddle-faddle,
You are wrong, they're all the same,
They're all the same.
I repeat that woman's constancy
Is the purest sort of fiction.

FERRANDO, GUGLIELMO

I believe in { Dorabella, } you can't
             { Fiordiligi }
weaken my conviction!

DON ALFONSO

Is that all you have to offer?

FERRANDO

Dorabella!

GUGLIELMO

Fiordiligi!

DON ALFONSO

Are you serious?

GUGLIELMO

Fiordiligi!

DON ALFONSO

Can you prove it?

FERRANDO

Dorabella!

DON ALFONSO

No, no, you can't!

FERRANDO

Dorabella!

GUGLIELMO

Fiordiligi!

DON ALFONSO

I say you can't!

RECITATIVE

FERRANDO

Theoretical bombast!

GUGLIELMO

The talk of senile cynics!

DON ALFONSO

I'm flattered! However, you say that
they are virtuous. Today that may
be true, but will it be tomorrow?
How can you be so certain? Have
you any guarantee that the love they
profess is eternal?

FERRANDO

Impeccable morals.

GUGLIELMO

Old-fashioned principles.

FERRANDO

Lofty ideals.

GUGLIELMO

Highminded way of life.

FERRANDO

Utter unselfishness.

GUGLIELMO

The firmest of characters!

FERRANDO

Her promise!

GUGLIELMO

Her honor!

FERRANDO

Her devotion!

DON ALFONSO

Kisses and tears, caresses, fits of swoon-
ing! What could be more ridiculous!

FERRANDO

Damnation! When will there be an end
to this?

DON ALFONSO

Be patient! What if I could convince
you this very day that they're like
all the others?

GUGLIELMO

That is a lie!

FERRANDO

Non è.

DON ALFONSO

Giochiam.

FERRANDO

Giochiamo.

DON ALFONSO

Cento zecchini.

GUGLIELMO

E mille, se volete.

DON ALFONSO

Parola.

FERRANDO

Parolissima.

DON ALFONSO

E un cenno, un motto, un gesto, giurate, di non far di tutto questo alle vostre Penelopi.

FERRANDO

Giuriamo.

DON ALFONSO

Da soldati d'onore.

GUGLIELMO

Da soldati d'onore.

DON ALFONSO

E tutto quel farete ch'io vi dirò di far.

FERRANDO

Tutto!

GUGLIELMO

Tuttissimo!

DON ALFONSO

Bravissimi!

FERRANDO, GUGLIELMO

Bravissimo! Signor Don Alfonsetto! A spese vostre or ci divertiremo. E de' cento zecchini, che faremo?

No. 3. TERZETTO

FERRANDO

Una bella serenata
far io voglio alla mia dea.

GUGLIELMO

In onor di Citerea
un convito io voglio far.

DON ALFONSO

Sarò anch'io de' convitati?

FERRANDO, GUGLIELMO

Ci sarete, si, Signor!

FERRANDO, DON ALFONSO, GUGLIELMO

E che brindis replicati
far vogliamo al Dio d'amor.

SCENE II

No. 4. DUETTO

FIORDILIGI

Ah guarda, sorella,
ah guarda, sorella,
se bocca più bella
se aspetto più nobile può ritrovar.

DORABELLA

Osserva tu un poco,
osserva che foco ha ne' sguardi,
se fiamma, se dardi sembran non scoccar.

FIORDILIGI

Si vede un sembiante
guerriero ed amante.

DORABELLA

Si vede una faccia,
che alletta, che alletta,
e minaccia.

FERRANDO

Of course!

DON ALFONSO

Will you bet?

FERRANDO

I'm willing.

DON ALFONSO

One hundred sovereigns!

GUGLIELMO

A thousand, if you wish!

DON ALFONSO

Agreed?

FERRANDO

On my honor!

DON ALFONSO

But promise: no inkling, no mention,
    not even a suggestion of our wager
    to your glorious paragons.

FERRANDO

We promise.

DON ALFONSO

On your honor as soldiers?

GUGLIELMO

On our honor as soldiers!

DON ALFONSO

And till tomorrow evening you will do
    what I say?

FERRANDO

Gladly!

GUGLIELMO

Most willingly!

DON ALFONSO

Your hand on it!

FERRANDO, GUGLIELMO

My hand on it! You connoisseur of
    women—

FERRANDO

To see you beaten will be extremely
    funny!

GUGLIELMO

(to Ferrando)

Let us plan how to spend all that
    money!

No. 3.   TERZET

FERRANDO

I shall serenade my goddess,
With a dozen fine musicians,
Sing her praises
In the honored old traditions.

GUGLIELMO

As the sure and happy winner
Of the bet we made before,
I shall give a gala dinner
For the sweetheart that I adore.

DON ALFONSO

May I also join the party?

FERRANDO, GUGLIELMO

Why of course, that's only fair!
Don Alfonso, you'll be there.

ALL THREE

While the sound of clinking glasses
Echoes gaily through the air,
We shall sing the endless praises
Of true women everywhere.

(Exeunt)

SCENE II

(A garden at the seashore. Fiordiligi
    and Dorabella, gazing at the portraits
    of their lovers in the little lockets
    they each wear.)

No. 4.   DUET

FIORDILIGI

See here, Dorabella,
Guglielmo, my lover!
Tell me, sister,
Where could you discover
So great a nobility
As shows in his face?

DORABELLA

This one of Ferrando,
I love it!
What light in his glances!
It sparkles, and dances
And lends him such grace!

FIORDILIGI

The face of a hero,
Audacious, yet disarming!

DORABELLA

His face is expressive,
So gracious, so kindly and charming.
Yet he's manly and possessive, so
    possessive!

FIORDILIGI

Felice son io!

DORABELLA

Io sono felice!

FIORDILIGI

Se questo mio core
mai cangia desio,
Amore mi faccia
vivendo penar.

DORABELLA

Se questo mi core
mai cangia desio,
Amore mi faccia
vivendo penar.

RECITATIVO

FIORDILIGI

Mi par, che stamattina volontieri
farei la pazzarella! ho un certo foco,
un certo pizzicor entro le vene —
quando Guglielmo viene — se sa-
pessi, che burla gli vo far.

DORABELLA

Per dirti il vero, qualche cosa di nuovo
anch' io nell' alma provo: io giurerei,
che lontane non siam da gli Imenei.

FIORDILIGI

Dammi la mano: io voglio astro-
logarti: uh, che bell' Emme! e
questo è un Pì: va bene: Matrimonio Presto.

DORABELLA

Affè, che ci avrei gusto.

FIORDILIGI

Ed io non ci avrei rabbia.

DORABELLA

Ma che diavol vuol dir che i nostri
sposi ritardano a venir? son già le
sei—

FIORDILIGI

Eccoli.

DORABELLA

Non son essi: è Don Alfonso, l'amico
lor.

SCENA III

FIORDILIGI

Ben venga il Signor Don Alfonso!

DON ALFONSO

Riverisco.

DORABELLA

Cos' è? perchè qui solo? voi piangete?
parlate per pietà! che cosa è nato?
d'amante—

FIORDILIGI

L'idol mio—

DON ALFONSO

Barbaro fato!

No. 5 ARIA

DON ALFONSO

Vorrei dir, e cor non ho, e cor non ho—
balbettando il labbro va—
fuor la voce uscir non può—
ma mi resta mezza quà.
Che farete?
Che farò?
oh che gran fatalità!
dar di peggio non si può, ah non si può,
ho di voi, di lor pietà.

RECITATIVO

FIORDILIGI

DON ALFONSO

Stelle! per carità, Signor Alfonso, non
ci fate morir.
Convien armarvi, figlie mie, di costanza.

BOTH

I'm ever so happy, contented and
  happy!
If this love of mine ever fails in affec-
  tion,
Or turns in another direction,
My darling, my darling,
May Fate take revenge on my heart!

DORABELLA

Beloved, may Fate take revenge on
  my heart.

FIORDILIGI

If ever my feelings should waver or
  alter,
If ever a discord should tear us apart,

BOTH

My darling, may Fate take revenge
  on my heart.

FIORDILIGI

Beloved, may Fate take revenge on
  my heart.

DORABELLA

If ever my candor should weaken or
  falter,
If ever my fervor should fail or depart,

BOTH

My darling, may Fate take revenge
  on my heart!

RECITATIVE

FIORDILIGI

Oh, such a lovely morning I can't help
  feeling just a little roguish. I can't
  explain it, but somehow I could do
  some harmless mischief. When my
  Guglielmo gets here, how I'd love
  to tease him just a bit!

DORABELLA

To be quite honest, I myself have a
  feeling that something's bound to
  happen. I almost think we are soon
  to be married to our sweethearts.

FIORDILIGI

Give me your hand, dear, I want to
  read your future. Look at that M
  there! And here a P! That's easy:
  Matrimony Pending!

DORABELLA

That's one thing I would welcome!

FIORDILIGI

I would not mind it either.

DORABELLA

But where in the world are our two
  sweethearts? What's keeping them
  so long? It's getting late.
  (enter Don Alfonso)

FIORDILIGI

There they are!

DORABELLA

You're mistaken, it's Don Alfonso,
  our mutual friend.

SCENE III

FIORDILIGI

Good morning to you, Don Alfonso.

DON ALFONSO

G-good morning!

DORABELLA

Dear me! you're out of breath and
  excited. For Heaven's sake, what's
  wrong? Can't you speak faster?
  Ferrando—?

FIORDILIGI

Guglielmo—?

DON ALFONSO

What a disaster!

No. 5 ARIA

How I hate to break the news!
It's so awful my lips refuse.
I must talk, I have no choice,
But it seems I've lost my voice.
How explain it? What to say?
Oh accursed, tragic day!
When you know, you will agree,
Nothing worse could ever be!
All your joys are done and past.
Poor dear boys, the die is cast.

RECITATIVE

FIORDILIGI

Goodness! What can it be, dear Don
  Alfonso? Do not keep us in suspense.

DON ALFONSO

You must have courage, be prepared
  for a shock.

DORABELLA

Oh Dei! qual male è addivenuto mai,
qual caso rio? forse è morto il mio
bene?

FIORDILIGI

È morto il mio?

DON ALFONSO

Morti non son, ma poco men che
morti.

DORABELLA

Feriti?

DON ALFONSO

No.

FIORDILIGI

Ammalati?

DON ALFONSO

Neppur.

FIORDILIGI

Che cosa dunque?

DON ALFONSO

Al marzial campo ordin regio li chiama.

FIORDILIGI, DORABELLA

Ohimè! che sento!

FIORDILIGI

E partiran?

DON ALFONSO

Sul fatto.

DORABELLA

E non v'è modo d'impedirlo?

DON ALFONSO

Non v'è.

FIORDILIGI

Ne un solo addio?

DON ALFONSO

Gli infelici non hanno coraggio di
vedervi; ma se voi lo bramate, son
pronti—

DORABELLA

Dove son?

DON ALFONSO

Amici, entrate!

No. 6   QUINTETTO

GUGLIELMO

Sento, o Dio!
che questo piede
è restio nel girle avante.

FERRANDO

Il mio labbro palpitante
non può detto pronunziar.

DON ALFONSO

Nei momenti i più terribili
sua virtù l'eroe palesa.

FIORDILIGI, DORABELLA

Or ch'abbbiam la nuova intesa,
a voi resta a fare il meno;
fate core, fate core,
a entrambe in seno
immergeteci l'acciar.

FERRANDO, GUGLIELMO

Idol mio! la sorte incolpa
se ti deggio abbandonar!

DORABELLA

Ah no, no, non partirai!

FIORDILIGI

No crudel, non tene andrai,

DORABELLA

Voglio pria cavarmi il core.

FIORDILIGI

Pria ti vo morire ai piedi.

FERRANDO

(Cosa dici?)

GUGLIELMO

(Te n'avveddi?)

DON ALFONSO

(Saldo amico, saldo amico,
finem lauda, finem lauda!)

FIORDILIGI, DORABELLA, FERRANDO,
DON ALFONSO, GUGLIELMO

Il destin così defrauda,
le speranze de' mortali.
Ah chi mai fra tanti mali,
chi mai può la vita amar?

DORABELLA

Good Heavens! What happened to our
fiancés? Are they in trouble? Is my
Ferrando dead?

FIORDILIGI

Or my Guglielmo?

DON ALFONSO

Dead—they are not, but not much
less than that.

DORABELLA

In prison?

DON ALFONSO

No.

FIORDILIGI

Are they ill?

DON ALFONSO

No, no.

FIORDILIGI

What could it be then?

DON ALFONSO

By royal order they must leave for the
front.

FIORDILIGI, DORABELLA

Oh dear! How dreadful!

FIORDILIGI

When do they leave?

DON ALFONSO

At once!

DORABELLA

And is there no way to exempt them?

DON ALFONSO

No way.

FIORDILIGI

And no good-byes?

DON ALFONSO

Wretched fellows, they don't have the
courage to face you. But if you
can both bear it, I'll call them.

DORABELLA

Oh, please do!

DON ALFONSO

Come in now, my heroes!

(*enter Ferrando and Guglielmo in
traveling clothes*)

No. 6. QUINTET

GUGLIELMO

All is over, the blow has fallen,
All my hopes destroyed and shattered.

FERRANDO

I am speechless, shocked and battered!
You behold a broken man!

DON ALFONSO

In the face of this catastrophe,
Steel your heart and be courageous!

FIORDILIGI, DORABELLA

Now that all has been decided,
You must do me one last favor:
Be a stoic, be heroic,
Without a waver
Plunge your sword right through my
heart.

FERRANDO, GUGLIELMO

Dearest angel! The worst has
happened!
Fate decrees that we must part.

DORABELLA

No, no, no, I cannot bear it!

FIORDILIGI

I will die of grief, I swear it!

DORABELLA

Let me perish, I implore you!

FIORDILIGI

Let me die right before you!

FERRANDO

(Are we winning?)

GUGLIELMO

(Are we losing?)

DON ALFONSO

(The beginning is amusing,
But tomorrow comes the sorrow!)

FIORDILIGI, DORABELLA

So does Fate take away the joy of
living,
End forever all the hopes and dreams
we cherished.

FERRANDO, DON ALFONSO, GUGLIELMO

So the sudden hand of Fate
Will take away the joy of living,
All the hopes and dreams we
cherished.

ALL

Bowed by grief, all alone in sorrow,
Who would care to live at all?

RECITATIVO

GUGLIELMO

Non piangere, idol mio!

FERRANDO

Non disperarti, adorata mia sposa!

DON ALFONSO

Lasciate lor tal sfogo: è troppo giusta
la cagion di quel pianto.

FIORDILIGI

Chi sa s'io più ti veggio?

DORABELLA

Chi sa se più ritorni?

FIORDILIGI

Lasciami questo ferro: ei mi dia morte,
se mai barbara sorte in quel seno a
me caro—

DORABELLA

Morrei di duol, d'uopo non ho d'acciaro.

FERRANDO, GUGLIELMO

Non farmi, anima mia, quest'infausti
presagi! proteggeran gli Dei la pace
del tuo cor ne'giorni miei.

No. 7. DUETTINO

FERRANDO, GUGLIELMO

Al fato dan legge
quegli occhi vezzosi;
Amor li protegge
nè i loro riposi
le barbare stelle ardiscon turbar.
Il ciglio sereno,
mio bene, a me gira;
felice al tuo seno
io spero tornar.

RECITATIVO

DON ALFONSO

(La comedia è graziosa, e tutti due
fan ben la loro parte.)

FERRANDO

O cielo! questo è il tamburo funesto.
che a divider mi vien dal mio tesoro.

DON ALFONSO

Ecco amici, la barca.

FIORDILIGI

Io manco.

DORABELLA

Io moro.

SCENA V

No. 8. CORO

Bella vita militar!
Ogni dì si cangia loco,
oggi molto, doman poco,
ora in terra ed or sul mar.
Il fragor di trombe e pifferi,
la sparar di schioppi, e bombe,
forza accresce al braccio, e all' anima
vaga sol di trionfar.
Bella vita militar!

RECITATIVO

DON ALFONSO

Non v'è più tempo, amici, andar conviene, ove il destino, anzi il dover
v'invita.

FIORDILIGI

Mio cor—

DORABELLA

Idolo mio—

FERRANDO

Mio ben—

GUGLIELMO

Mia vita—

FIORDILIGI

Ah per un sol momento—

DON ALFONSO

Del vostro reggimento già è partita la
barca, raggiungerla convien coi pocchi amici che su legno più lieve attendendo vi stanno.

FERRANDO, GUGLIELMO

Abbracciami, idol mio!

FIORDILIGI, DORABELLA

Muojo d'affanno.

RECITATIVE

GUGLIELMO

Take courage, my beloved!

FERRANDO

My little sweetheart, do not yield to despair.

DON ALFONSO

My friends, you must be patient, do not console them, let them have a good cry.

FIORDILIGI

Perhaps we part forever!

DORABELLA

How can I live without you!

(they embrace tenderly)

FIORDILIGI

Lend me your sword, I beg you, to end my torture. Since fortune is so cruel, only death can console me!

DORABELLA

I'll die of grief, I shall not need a weapon.

FERRANDO, GUGLIELMO

Forget these ominous fancies, and remember, I love you! Trust to the gods above you, to cheer your grieving heart, and guide me safely.

No. 7. DUETTINO

FERRANDO, GUGLIELMO

Your love is a power,
An ally beside us;
A beacon, a tower,
A star that will guide us;
The barbarous fates too must bow to
  its reign.
So wait and be patient;
No space can divide us.
We'll soon be united and happy again.

RECITATIVE

DON ALFONSO

(The performance is charming! The way they're acting exceeds my expectations!)

(a drum is heard)

FERRANDO

Oh Heavens! That is the ominous signal, which will tear me away from my beloved.

DON ALFONSO

And the boat is arriving.

FIORDILIGI

Guglielmo!

DORABELLA

Ferrando!

SCENE V

(Enter soldies, village men and women. The military march is heard in the distance. A boat arrives at the landing.)

No. 8. CHORUS

On to glory, on to war!
We are free of care and sorrow,
Here today and there tomorrow!
Over land and over sea!
We are marching on to victory
With the flags and banners flying
For our country's honor,
While trumpets are sounding
And our spirits soar.
On to glory, on to war!

RECITATIVE

DON ALFONSO

My friends, it's time you started. You must be going, duty is calling, destiny has decided.

FIORDILIGI

My love—

DORABELLA

My dear beloved—

FERRANDO

My life—

GUGLIELMO

My treasure—

FIORDILIGI

Stay just a moment longer!

DON ALFONSO

The first one of the barges has already departed. Hurry to meet the soldiers who are waiting to escort you on board. They are getting impatient.

FERRANDO, GUGLIELMO

Just one last kiss, my darling!

FIORDILIGI, DORABELLA

I cannot bear it!

No. 9. QUINTETTO

FIORDILIGI

Di scrivermi ogni giorno!
giurami, vita mia!

DORABELLA

Due volte ancora tu
'scrivimi, se puoi.

FERRANDO

Sii certa, sii certa,
o cara!

GUGLIELMO

Non dubitar,
non dubitar, mio bene!

DON ALFONSO

Io crepo se non rido.

FIORDILIGI

Sii costante a me sol!

DORABELLA

Serbati fido!

FERRANDO

Addio!

GUGLIELMO

Addio!

FIORDILIGI, DORABELLA

Addio!

FIORDILIGI, DORABELLA, FERRANDO,
GUGLIELMO

Mi si divide il cor,
bell' idol mio!
Addio!

CORO

Bella vita militar, ecc.

SCENA VI

RECITATIVO

DORABELLA

Dove son?

DON ALFONSO

Son partiti.

FIORDILIGI

Oh dipartenza crudelissima amara!

DON ALFONSO

Fate core, carissime figliuole; guardate,
da lontano vi fan cenno con mano i
cari sposi.

FIORDILIGI

Buon viaggio. Mia vita!

DORABELLA

Buon viaggio!

FIORDILIGI

Oh Dei! come veloce se ne va quella
barca! già sparisce! già non si vede
più. Deh faccia il cielo ch'abbia
prospero corso.

DORABELLA

Faccia che al campo giunga con fortu-
nati auspici.

DON ALFONSO

E a voi salvi gli amanti, e a me gli
amici.

No. 10. TERZETTINO

FIORDILIGI, DORABELLA, DON ALFONSO

Soave sia il vento,
tranquilla sia l'onda,
ed ogni elemento
benigno risponda
ai nostri desir!

SCENA VII

RECITATIVO

DON ALFONSO

Non son cattivo comico! va bene; al
concertato loco i due campioni di
Ciprigna, e di Marte mi staranno attendendo; or senza indugio, raggiun-
gerli conviene. Quante smorfie, quante buffonerie! Tanta meglio per me,
cadran più facilmente: questa razza
di gente è la più presto a cangiarsi
d'umore. Oh poverini! per femmina
giocar cento zecchini?

No. 9.   Quintet

FIORDILIGI
(weeping)
Be sure to write me daily,
Ev'ry day, will you promise?
Swear you'll always be true!

DORABELLA
(weeping)
You write me twice a day.
Twice daily, please, will you?

FERRANDO
Of course, dear, I promise, dear angel.

GUGLIELMO
Of course I will.
I promise, my dear angel.

DON ALFONSO
(aside)
This really is too silly!

FIORDILIGI
Swear you'll always be true!

DORABELLA
Think of me always!

FERRANDO
I promise!

GUGLIELMO
I promise!

FIORDILIGI, DORABELLA
Farewell, then!

FIORDILIGI, DORABELLA, FERRANDO,
GUGLIELMO
How I shall grieve and mourn
When we are parted!
I love you,
Forever, forever!
(Ferrando and Guglielmo board the boat. The two women stand at the landing, motionless. The boat gradually recedes in the distance, to the sound of drums.)

CHORUS
On to glory, on to war! etc.
(exit chorus)

SCENE VI

RECITATIVE

DORABELLA
(as if awakening from a trance)
Are they gone?

DON ALFONSO
They are gone.

FIORDILIGI
This separation is a terrible blow!

DON ALFONSO
Be courageous, it's not as bad as that.
Look there, now; in the distance, on the ship you can see your sweethearts waving.

FIORDILIGI
God keep you, my treasure.

DORABELLA
Safe journey!

FIORDILIGI
How rapidly the vessel disappears in the distance! In one moment they will be out of sight. Heaven protect them on their perilous journey!

DORABELLA
How I will miss my darling, away in foreign lands!

DON ALFONSO
I will miss them no less—my two best friends.

No. 10.   Terzettino

FIORDILIGI, DORABELLA, DON ALFONSO
May breezes blow lightly,
May fair winds betide you,
May stars shimmer brightly
And faithfully guide you,
Beloved so dear.
May Fortune direct you
And journey beside you,
Watch over and protect you,
Benign and responsive
To love so sincere.
(exeunt Fiordiligi and Dorabella)

SCENE VII

RECITATIVE

DON ALFONSO
I have a flair for comedy! My acting, to judge from my success, has been convincing. But Fernando and Guglielmo, can they equal my performance? I'll go and meet them to coach them for their roles. And the ladies! Much ado about nothing. That means only one thing: they'll weaken so much sooner. They're the kind of women who are quickest to reverse their affection. Oh you poor fellows! You risk a hundred sov'-reigns on two women!

Nel mare solca,
e nell' arena semina,
e il vago vento
spera in rete accogliere
chi fonda sue speranze
in cor di femmina.

No. 11. RECITATIVO ED ARIA

DORABELLA

Ah scostati! paventa il tristo effetto
d'un disperato affetto. Chiudi quelle
finestre—odio la luce, odio l'aria, che
spiro—odio me stessa! Chi schernisce
il mio duol? chi mi consola? Deh
fuggi, per pietà! fuggi, lasciami sola.

SCENA VIII

RECITATIVO

DESPINA

Che vita maledetta è il far la cameriera! dal mattino alla sera si fa, si
suda, si lavora, e poi di tanto, che
si fa, nulla è per noi. E mezza ora,
che sbatto, il cioccolatte è fatto,
ed a me tocca restar ad odorarlo a
secca bocca? non è forse la mia
come la vostra? o garbate Signore,
che a voi dessi l'essenza e a me
l'odore? per Bacco, vo assagiarlo:
com' è buono! Vien gente! oh ciel!
son le padrone.

ARIA

Smanie implacabili,
che m'agitate,
entro quest' anima
più non cessate,
finchè l'angoscia
mi fa morir.

Esempio misero
d'amor funesto,
darò all' Eumenidi,
se viva resto
col suono orribile
de' miei sospir,
col suono orrible
de' miei sospir.

SCENA IX

DESPINA
Madame, ecco la vostra collazione.
Diamine! cosa fate?

FIORDILIGI
Ah!

DORABELLA
Ah!

DESPINA
Che cosa è nato?

FIORDILIGI
Ov' è un acciaro?

DORABELLA
un veleno, dov è?

DESPINA
Padrone, dico!

RECITATIVO

DESPINA
Signora Dorabella, Signora Fiordiligi,
ditemi, che cosa è stato?

DORABELLA
Oh terribil disgrazia!

DESPINA
Sbrigatevi in buon' ora.

FIORDILIGI
Da Napoli partiti sono gli amanti
nostri.

DESPINA
Non c'è altro? ritorneran.

A man in danger,
Lost in the jungle's wilderness
Or in a shipwreck,
Is safer than the simpleton
Who founds his hopes on woman
And her fidelity.

(*Curtain*)

SCENE VIII

(*A pretty room, with several chairs, a little table, three doors. Despina alone.*)

RECITATIVE

DESPINA

There's nothing quite so thankless as being a perfect maid. From morning till midnight you work, you slave, do your best, and when you're finished, you have nothing to show for it. For example, I have to serve my mistresses' breakfast and all I get is the wonderful aroma of fresh coffee. Do they want me to live on mere aroma? Just where is it written that they should have the egg and I the shell? For once I think, I'll try some. How delicious.
(*she wipes her mouth*)
The ladies! That was a narrow escape!

SCENE IX

(*enter Fiordiligi and Dorabella, distraught*)

My ladies, I've already brought your breakfast. Bless my soul! What has happened?

FIORDILIGI
Ah!

DORABELLA
Ah!

DESPINA
What's the matter?

FIORDILIGI
Find me a dagger!

DORABELLA
And some poison for me!

DESPINA
My ladies, easy!

No. 11. RECITATIVE AND ARIA

DORABELLA

Away from here! For in my state of frenzy I might do something desp'-rate. You must draw all the curtains —I hate the sunlight, hate the air I am breathing, even myself! Who would mock my despair? Who dares console me? Away from me at once! Hurry, hurry! Far from where I am! Leave me alone here!

Come, endless agony,
Come and possess me,
Enter this heart of mine,
Burn and obsess me,
Torment and goad me
Until I die.

My love is tragedy
With none to share it.
Should cruel destiny
Force me to bear it,
Till death releases me,
I'll mourn and sigh.
Come, hopeless misery,
Deride and taunt me,
Enter this soul of mine,
Pursue and haunt me,
Pierce and corrode me
Until I die.
My love is martyrdom,
A storm that rages.
Should Fate prolong my life
Through countless ages,
I'll grieve the years away
Until I die.

(*both women collapse in their chairs, in utter despair*)

RECITATIVE

DESPINA

Dear mistress Dorabella, dear mistress Fiordiligi, tell me, what has happened?

DORABELLA
A terrible disaster!

DESPINA
Please tell me about it.

FIORDILIGI
Our fiancés left Naples and we are both deserted!

DESPINA
Oh, is that all? They will be back.

DORABELLA

Chi sa!

DESPINA

Come, chi sa? dove son iti?

DORABELLA

Al campo di battaglia.

DESPINA

Tanto meglio per loro: li vedrete
tornar carchi d'alloro.

FIORDILIGI

Ma ponno anche perir.

DESPINA

Allora poi tanto meglio per voi.

FIORDILIGI

Sciocca, che dici?

DESPINA

La pura verità: due ne perdete, vi
restan tutti gli altri.

FIORDILIGI

Ah, perdendo Guglielmo, mi pare
ch'io morrei!

DORABELLA

Ah, Ferrando perdendo, mi par, che
viva a sepellirmi andrei.

DESPINA

Brave, vi par, ma non è ver: ancora
non vi fu donna, ch'è d'amor sia
morta. Per un uomo morir! altri, ve
n'hanno, che compensano il danno.

DORABELLA

E credi che potria altro uom amar,
chi s'ebbe per amante un Guglielmo,
un Ferrando?

DESPINA

Han gli altri ancora tutto quello ch'han
essi, un uom adesso amate, un altro
n'amerete, uno val l'altro, perchè
nessun val nulla; ma non parliam
di ciò, sono ancor vivi, e vivi torneran; ma son lontani, e più tosto
che in vani pianti perdere il tempo,
pensate a divertivi.

FIORDILIGI

Divertirci?

DESPINA

Sicuro! e quel ch'è meglio far all' amor
come assassine, e come faranno al
campo i vostri cari amanti.

DORABELLA

Non offender così quelle alme belle,
di fedeltà, d'intatto amore esempi.

DESPINA

Via, via, passaro i tempi di spacciar
queste favole ai bambini.

No. 12.   ARIA

DESPINA

In uomini
In soldati
sperare fedeltà?
In uomini
sperare fedeltà?
In soldati
sperare fedeltà?
Non vi fate sentir per carità!
Non vi fate sentir per carità!

Di pasta simile son tutti quanti,
son tutti quanti.
han più degli uomini stabilità.

Mentite lagrime,
fallaci sguardi,
voci ingannevoli,
vezzi bugiardi,
son le primarie
lor qualità.
In noi non amano che il cor diletto,
poi ci dispregiano, neganci affetto,
nè val da' barbari chieder pietà.

Paghiam, a femmine, d'ugual moneta
questa malefica razza indiscreta;
amiam per comodo, per vanità.

DORABELLA

Who knows?

DESPINA

Why do you say that? Where have they gone?

DORABELLA

They have both gone to war.

DESPINA

So much the better! In that case they'll return covered with laurels.

FIORDILIGI

But if they should die?

DESPINA

Well, what about it? All the better for you!

FIORDILIGI
(rises in rage)

How dare you say that!

DESPINA

I merely tell the truth. What if you lose them? There still are all the others.

FIORDILIGI

Ah, without my Guglielmo I could not go on living!

DORABELLA

Ah, if I would lose Ferrando, then for me also death would be more than welcome.

DESPINA

Well spoken indeed, but you are wrong. I've never heard of a woman dying of love. To die for a man, when a thousand others can be had for the asking!

DORABELLA

You really mean to tell me that there are men comparing even vaguely with a Guglielmo, a Ferrando?

DESPINA

They are no better, nor are they worse than the others. Today you're loving one man, tomorrow another. One's worth the others, because they are all worthless! Why waste your time on tears? They're still alive, and will be for some time. But they're away and rather than lament in sackcloth and ashes, forget them and be gay.

FIORDILIGI
(furiously)

Forget them?

DESPINA

Exactly! By far the best cure for lonely hearts is a new romance. What else do you think your sweethearts are doing while they're away?

DORABELLA

You dare to offend those noble spirits, models of faith and paragons of virtue?

DESPINA

You think that men are stable? That's no more than an old woman's fable!

No. 12. Aria

DESPINA

Stability in a soldier
And virtue in a man?
Who ever saw it since the world began?
Give me one good example if you can
If you can!
(laughing)
Who'd believe such a sentimental tale
Of the perfect and ever-loving male!
Dealing with woman kind, all men are
    brothers—
One like the others!
Don't be a featherbrain
Ever to trust them.
Even a weather-vane changes much
    less.
All men's duplicity
Passes believing.
Feigning simplicity,
Lying, deceiving,
And when they fool you, oh what
    finesse!
Let him be glamorous,
Clever and handsome,
Gallant and amorous,
Stronger than Samson!
Do not be gullible,
Trusting his lies!
He wants to pull the wool
Over your eyes,
Your trusting eyes!
Pay them in kind when they flirt and
    philander.
Sauce for the goose is the same for the
    gander!
Even the best of them,

SCENA X

RECITATIVO

DON ALFONSO

Che silenzio! che aspetto di tristezza
spirano queste stanze! Poverette! non
han già tutto il torto: bisogna consolarle; infin che vanno i due creduli
sposi, com' io loro commisi, a mas-
cherasi, pensiam cosa può farsi —
temo un po' per Despina,—quella
furba potrebbe riconoscerli; potrebbe
rovesciarmi le macchine, vedremo—
se mai farà bisogno un regaletto a
tempo, un zechinetto per una cam-
eriere è un gran scongiuro. Ma per
esser sicuro, si potria metterla in
parte a parte del secreto. Excellente
è il progetto—la sua camera è questa
—Despinetta!

DESPINA

Chi batte?

DON ALFONSO

Oh!

DESPINA

Ih!

DON ALFONSO

Despina mia, di te bisogno avrei.

DESPINA

Ed io niente di voi.

DON ALFONSO

Ti vo fare del ben.

DESPINA

A una fanciulla un vecchio come lei
non può far nulla.

DON ALFONSO

Parla piano ed osserva.

DESPINA

Me lo dona?

DON ALFONSO

Sì, se meco sei buona.

DESPINA

E che vorebbe? è loro il mio giulebbe.

DON ALFONSO

Ed oro avrai; ma ci vuol fedeltà.

DESPINA

Non c'è altro? son quà.

DON ALFONSO

Prendi ed ascolta. Sai, che le tue
padrone han perduti gli amanti.

DESPINA

Lo so.

DON ALFONSO

Tutti i lor pianti, tutti deliri loro
ancor tu sai.

DESPINA

So tutto.

DON ALFONSO

Or ben; se mai per consolarle un poco,
e trar, come diciam, chiodo per
chiodo, tu ritrovassi il modo, da
metter in lor grazia due soggetti di
garbo che vorrieno provar, già mi
capisci. C'è una mancia per te di
venti scudi, se li fai riuscir.

DESPINA

Non mi dispiace questa proposizione.
Ma con quelle buffone . . . basta,
udite: son giovani? son belli? e sopra
tutto hanno una buona borsa i vostri
concorrenti?

DON ALFONSO

Han tutto quello che piacer può alle
donne di giudizio. Li vuoi veder?

DESPINA

E dove son?

'Neath his veneer
Is like the rest of them,
Never you fear!
Perish the thought of a man who is
  true,
Do unto them as they do unto you!
  (*exeunt. Enter Don Alfonso*)

SCENE X

RECITATIVE

DON ALFONSO

Not a sound! This atmosphere of sadness! Graver than a grave-yard. Poor girls! They must be very downcast! I cannot really blame them. Meanwhile, I'll go and meet my two friends. In their present disguise I'm optimistic my strategy is foolproof! But that rascal Despina! She is clever —she might see through the masquerade. She even might upset the whole applecart! However . . . I know just how to handle a girl like Despina. A little money always goes a long way in such a case. But to further my purpose, I could even ask her to be a partner in my project. Without losing a minute I will knock at her door.
  (*knocks*)
Despinetta!

DESPINA

Who's knocking?

DON ALFONSO

I!

DESPINA
  (*entering*)
Oh!

DON ALFONSO

My dear Despina, I want to ask a favor.

DESPINA

I don't give any favors!

DON ALFONSO

Won't you listen to my offer?

DESPINA

To girls of my age, a man of your vintage offers very little.

DON ALFONSO
  (*shows her a gold piece*)
This might change your opinion.

DESPINA

A gold piece?

DON ALFONSO

Yes. It's yours for the asking.

DESPINA

What are you asking? For gold I might do it.

DON ALFONSO

The merest trifle—your good-will and your help.

DESPINA

Is that all? Go on.

DON ALFONSO

Well, then, here's my problem. Doubtlessly you have heard what has happened to your ladies?

DESPINA

I have.

DON ALFONSO

Then you have noticed that they are overcome by desperation.

DESPINA

What about it?

DON ALFONSO

Now then: suppose, in order to distract them, or, as the saying goes, make the best of a bad bargain, you help me to persuade them to meet two nice young men with romantic intentions, who are here from abroad. You understand me, if you make them successful, I shall give you a most generous reward.

DESPINA

That sounds appealing. It's an attractive proposition. But those two silly females! — Tell me — your visitors, these foreigners, are they handsome? And, more important, have they well-lined pockets—these two prospective lovers?

DON ALFONSO

They are the most eligible young men any women could dream of! Is that enough?

DESPINA

Where are they now?

DON ALFONSO
Son lì: li posso far entrar?

DESPINA
Direi di sì.

SCENE XI

No. 13. Sestetto

DON ALFONSO
Alla bella Despinetta
vi presento, amici miei;
non dipende che da lei,
consolar il vostro cor.

FERRANDO, GUGLIELMO
Per la man,
che lieto io bacio,
per quei rai di grazia pieni,
fa che volga a me sereni
i begli occhi il mio tesor.

DESPINA
Che sembianze!
che vestiti!
che figure!
che mustacchi!
Io non so,
se son Vallacchi?
o se Turchi
son costor?
Vallacchi?
Turchi?
Turchi?
Vallacchi?

DON ALFONSO
Che ti par di quell' aspetto?

DESPINA
Per parlarvi schietto, schietto,
hanno un muso fuor dell'uso,
vero antidoto d'amor.
Che figure, che mustacchi!
Io non so, se son Vallacchi?
O se Turchi
son costor?

FERRANDO, DON ALFONSO, GUGLIELMO
Or la cosa è appien decisa,
se costei non ci ravvisa,
non c'è più nessun timor.

FIORDILIGI, DORABELLA
Ehi, Despina! olà Despina!

DESPINA
Le padrone.

DON ALFONSO
Ecco l'istante!
fa con arte:
io qui m'ascondo.

FIORDILIGI, DORABELLA
Ragazzaccia tracotante!
che fai lì con simil gente,
con simil gente?
falli uscire immantinente,
o ti so pentir con lor.

DESPINA, FERRANDO, GUGLIELMO
Ah, madame, perdonate!
al bel piè languir mirate
due meschin, di vostro merto,
spasimanti adorator.

FIORDILIGI, DORABELLA
Giusti numi! cosa sento?
dell' enorme tradimento,
chi fu mai l'indegno autor?

DESPINA, FERRANDO, GUGLIELMO
Deh calmate,
deh calmate,
quello sdegno.

FIORDILIGI, DORABELLA
Ah, che più non ho ritegno!
tutta piena ho l'alma in petto
di dispetto e di terror!

DON ALFONSO
Right here. May I ask them in?

DESPINA
A good· idea!
(*Don Alfonso opens the door and the disguised lovers step in*)

SCENE XI

No. 13. SEXTET

DON ALFONSO
I present Miss Despinetta,
A discreet and charming person.
There is no one who knows better
How to help you reach your goal.

FERRANDO, GUGLIELMO
I am pleased and deeply honored
At the compliment you paid me,
Being kind enough to aid me
Win the goddess of my soul.

DESPINA
(*laughing to herself*)
Goodness gracious!
How loquacious!
That regalia! Those mustaches!
Did they come here from Patagonia
Or perhaps from Timbuctoo?
The Congo? China? Turkey? Malaya?

DON ALFONSO
(*softly to Despina*)
Don't you think they have some
  virtue?

DESPINA
Though I do not like to hurt you,
They're fantastic,
Far too drastic,
And as lovers, they won't do!
Too outlandish, too exotic,
Positively Don Quixotic.
I am quite surprised at you.
Don Alfonso, just between us,
Did you find them on the moon
Or perhaps on Mars or Venus,
Did they land in a balloon?

FERRANDO, DON ALFONSO, GUGLIELMO
She is fooled by our (their) disguises!
Barring unforeseen surprises,
There is nothing more to fear.

FIORDILIGI, DORABELLA
(*from within*)
Eh, Despina! Come here, Despina!

DESPINA
I am coming!

DON ALFONSO
(*to Despina*)
Now, you take over, and remember,
I'll join you later.
(*He retires. Enter Fiordiligi and Dorabella.*)

FIORDILIGI, DORABELLA
I must say this is the limit!
You're forgetting your position.
Who has given you permission
To indulge in silly babble
With total strangers and common
  rabble?
Put the creatures out the door,
Nothing less and nothing more!

DESPINA, FERRANDO, GUGLIELMO
(*All three kneel down.*)
Ah, dear ladies, how unfeeling!
Here before your feet are kneeling
Two poor slaves, begging your mercy,
That is all we're asking for.

FIORDILIGI, DORABELLA
What an outrage. What pretensions!
Who would force unwished attentions
On us now, amid our woe?
Who would dare descend so low?

DESPINA, FERRANDO, GUGLIELMO
Dearest ladies, they (we) are gentle,
Sentimental!

FIORDILIGI, DORABELLA
Now I'm thoroughly disgusted,
You are brazen and revolting!
Stop molesting us and go!

DESPINA, DON ALFONSO
(*the latter from the doorway*)
I've a certain strong suspicion
That their fury is all for show.

FERRANDO, GUGLIELMO
I am certain their opposition
And their fury is not for show.

FIORDILIGI, DORABELLA
Ah, dear love, the pangs I suffer
You will never, never know.
You are brazen and revolting
With the insults you propose.

DESPINA

Mi da un poco
di sospetto,
quella rabbia
e quel furor!

DON ALFONSO

Mi da un poco
di sospetto,
quella rabbia
e quel furor!

FERRANDO

Qual diletto
è a questo petto,
quella rabbia
e quel furor!

GUGLIELMO

Qual diletto
è a questo petto,
quella rabbia
e quel furor!

FIORDILIGI

Ah, perdon
mio bel diletto,
innocente
è questo cor.

DORABELLA

Ah, perdon
mio bel diletto,
innocente
è questo cor.

RECITATIVO

DON ALFONSO

Che susurro! che strepito, che scompiglio è mai questo! siete pazze, care le mie ragazze? volete sollevar il vicinato? cosa avete? ch' è nato?

DORABELLA

Oh ciel! mirate uomini in casa nostra?

DON ALFONSO

Che male c'è?

FIORDILIGI

Che male? in questo giorno?
dopo il caso funesto?

DON ALFONSO

Stelle! sogno, o son desto? amici miei, miei dolcissimi amici! Voi quì? come? perchè? quando! in qual modo! Numi! quanto ne godo! (Secondatemi.)

FERRANDO

Amico Don Alfonso!

GUGLIELMO

Amico caro!

DON ALFONSO

Oh, bella improvisata!

DESPINA

Li conoscete voi?

DON ALFONSO

Se li conosco! questi sono i più dolci amici, ch'io m'abbia in questo mondo, e vostri ancor saranno.

FIORDILIGI

E in casa mia che fanno?

GUGLIELMO

Ai vostri piedi due rei, due delinquenti, ecco Madame! Amor—

FIORDILIGI

Numi! che sento?

FERRANDO

Amor, il nume, si possente per voi, qui ci conduce.

GUGLIELMO

Vista appena la luce di vostre fulgidissime pupille—

FERRANDO

che alle vive faville—

DESPINA, DON ALFONSO

I am sure they won't stay faithful
And their fury is a pose.

FERRANDO, GUGLIELMO

I am certain they are faithful
And their fury is no pose.

FIORDILIGI, DORABELLA

We are thoroughly disgusted.

DESPINA, DON ALFONSO, FERRANDO,
GUGLIELMO

Their resentment can't (can) be
trusted
And this fury is a (no) pose.

FIORDILIGI, DORABELLA

I refuse to stay and listen
To the insults you propose.

DESPINA, DON ALFONSO

I've a certain strong suspicion
That this fury is all a pose.

FERRANDO, GUGLIELMO

How I relish the opposition
That this fury so clearly shows.

FIORDILIGI, DORABELLA

What a shameless imposition!
Your offensive proposition
Only adds to all our woes.

FERRANDO, GUGLIELMO

Their behavior is an admission
They are faithful as we suppose.

DESPINA, DON ALFONSO

I am nursing a suspicion
They're pretending as we suppose.

FIORDILIGI, DORABELLA

Stop molesting us and go,
We will spite you until you go,

DON ALFONSO, DESPINA

They will spite you until you go.

FERRANDO, GUGLIELMO

They will spite us until we go.

ALL

And the answer will be No!

RECITATIVE

DON ALFONSO
(entering)

What commotion! What excitement!
And why all this confusion? My
dear ladies, have you lost your
minds? You're liable to rouse all
the neighbors! What has happened,
I ask you?

DORABELLA
(furiously)

Good Lord! An outrage! Men in a
house like ours!

DON ALFONSO

Is that so bad?

FIORDILIGI
(enraged)

So bad? It is unheard of—on this
tragic occasion!

DON ALFONSO

Bless me! It can't be. Am I dreaming?
I can't believe it! My two very best
friends! You here? Really? How so?
You here! Of all people! Tell me,
when did you get here? (Play along
with me!)
(they rapturously embrace each other)

FERRANDO

I'm overjoyed to see you!

GUGLIELMO

My benefactor!

DON ALFONSO

What a·very small world!

DESPINA

You've seen these men before?

DON ALFONSO

Oh, have I seen them! I have known
them since they were babies! I love
them like a father, and you will love
them also.

FIORDILIGI

What do they want in my house?

GUGLIELMO

Two humble creatures, two slaves, two
wretched wretches, lie at your feet
here, and love—

FIORDILIGI

Heavens! How dare you!
(the women draw back, weakly, followed by the persistent lovers.)

FERRANDO

And Love, our idol, leads us onward
to you, into your power.

GUGLIELMO

Overcome by your beauty, the devas-
tating splendor of your eyes—

FERRANDO

Like two fluttering butterflies—

GUGLIELMO
farfallette amorose e agonizzanti—

FERRANDO
vi voliamo davanti—

GUGLIELMO
ed ai lati ed a retro—

FERRANDO, GUGLIELMO
per implorar pietade in flebil metro!

FIORDILIGI
Stelle! che ardir!

DORABELLA
Sorella! che facciamo?

No. 14. RECITATIVO ED ARIA

FIORDILIGI
Temerari, sortite fuori di questo loco!
e non profani l'alito infausto degli
infami detti nostro cor, nostro
orecchio, e nostri affetti! Invan per
voi, per gli altri invan si cerca le
nostre alme sedur: l'intatta fede che
per noi già si diede ai cari amanti
saprem loro serbar infino a morte, a
dispetto del mondo e della sorte.

ARIA

Come scoglio immoto resta
contra i venti e la tempesta,
così ognor quest' alma è forte
nella fede e nell' amor.

Con noi nacque quella face,
che ci piace, e ci consola;
e potrà la morte sola,
far che cangi affetto il cor.
Come soglio immoto resta
contra i venti e la tempesta
così ognor quest'alma è forte
nella fede e nell' amor.

Rispettate, anime ingrate,
questo esempio di costanza,
e una barbara speranza
non vi renda audaci ancor.

RECITATIVO

FERRANDO
Ah, non partite!

GUGLIELMO
Ah, barbara restate! (Che vi pare?)

DON ALFONSO
(Aspettate!) Per carità ragazze, non
mi fate più far trista figura.

DORABELLA
E che pretendereste?

DON ALFONSO
Eh nulla; ma mi pare che un pocchin
di dolcezza — alfin son galantuomini
e sono amici miei.

FIORDILIGI
Come! e udire dovrei?

GUGLIELMO
Le nostre pene e sentirne pietà! La
celeste beltà degli occhi vostri la
piaga aprì nei nostri cui rimediar può
solo il balsamo d'amore: un solo
istante il core aprite o bella a sue
dolci facelle, a voi davanti spirar
vedrete i più fedeli amanti.

No. 15. ARIA

GUGLIELMO
Non siate ritrosi
occhietti vezzosi,
due lampi amorosi
vibrate un po' quà.
Felici rendeteci
amate con noi,
e noi felicissimi
faremo anche voi.

Guardate, toccate,
Il tutto osservate:
siam forti e ben fatti,
e come ognun vede,
sia merito, sia caso.
abbiamo bel piede,
bell' occhio, bel naso,
guardate bel piede,
osservate bell'occhio,

GUGLIELMO
Irresistibly drawn into your orbit—

FERRANDO
Like two bees by two rosebuds—

GUGLIELMO
There we hover, adoring,

BOTH
And humbly ask for mercy and consolation!

FIORDILIGI
That is enough!

DORABELLA
O sister, what to do now?

No. 14.   RECITATIVE AND ARIA

FIORDILIGI
Bold intruders, leave this house this
    very instant.
    (*Despina becomes alarmed*)
We will not let you profane our ears,
our spirits' inmost reaches, with
your vile, sacrilegious, disgusting
speeches! Do not attempt to win
our love or ever find the way to
our hearts. Our faith is lasting and
belongs now and always to our be-
loveds, till the day of our death,
pure and unfailing, in the face of
misfortune ever prevailing.

Strongly founded, a marble tower,
Safely guarded from ev'ry foe
    and hostile power,
So my heart, forever faithful,
Bears an armor no force can rend.

It is love, complete, unfailing
Bringing joy and sweetest comfort,
Over evil force prevailing,
Forever prevailing,
Love that only death can end.
Strongly founded, a marble tower,
    etc.

You will never win our favor.
Bear the truth with resignation.
We are proof against temptation,
We are deaf when you implore.
Cast your idle hopes away.
There is nothing more to say.
We are faithful evermore,
For evermore!

(*the women start to leave. Ferrando
and Guglielmo try to detain them.*)

RECITATIVE

FERRANDO
Please do not leave us!

GUGLIELMO
(*to Dorabella*)
How can you be so cruel!
(*to Alfonso*)
(See, I told you!)

DON ALFONSO
(Wait till later.) Dear ladies, I implore you, your outbursts embarass
me severely.

DORABELLA
(*angrily*)
Just what are you suggesting?

DON ALFONSO
Quite simply: there's no reason to become so offensive. They are not only
gentlemen, but also friends of mine.

FIORDILIGI
Really! And why should we listen?

GUGLIELMO
Because we're suffering and deserve
to be heard. The heavenly radiance
of your beauty has thrown us into
misery for which there is no remedy
except the balm of love. Just for
one moment bestow on us the favor
of your merciful pity! You see us
lying abjectly before you. Our passion is undying!

No. 15.   ARIA

GUGLIELMO
How can you refuse us
The light of your gazes,
The glow that suffuses
And dazes our hearts?
We promise you happiness
Untroubled by sadness,
A life that is paradise,
All sunshine and gladness!
Have patience, consider our
    qualifications:
We're strong and athletic,
Romantic, poetic,
We're just over twenty,
With money a-plenty,
And so sympathetic,
Good-natured and healthy,
Well-balanced and wealthy,

toccate bel naso,
il tutto osservate:
e questi mustacchi
chiamare si possono
trionfi degli uomini,
penacchi d'amor,
trionfi,
penacchi, mustacchi!

SCENA XII

No. 16. TERZETTO

DON ALFONSO

E voi ridete?

FERRANDO, GUGLIELMO

Certo, ridiamo.

DON ALFONSO

Ma cosa avete?

FERRANDO, GUGLIELMO

Già lo sappiamo.

DON ALFONSO

Ridete piano.

FERRANDO, GUGLIELMO

Parlate invano.

DON ALFONSO

Ridete piano,
piano,
piano,
piano.

FERRANDO, GUGLIELMO

Parlate invano,
Parlate invano.

DON ALFONSO

Se vi sentissero,
se vi scoprissero,
si guasterebbe
tutto l'affar,
si guasterebbe
tutto l'affar.

FERRANDO, GUGLIELMO

Ah che dal ridere,

DON ALFONSO

Mi fa da ridere

FERRANDO, GUGLIELMO

l'alma dividere,
ah, ah, ah, ah, ah, ah, ah, ah,

DON ALFONSO

questo lor ridere,
ma so che in piangere
dee terminar.

FERRANDO, GUGLIELMO

Ah, che dal ridere
l'alma dividere,
Ah, ah, ah, ah!
Ah, che le viscere
sento scoppiar.

DON ALFONSO

Mi da da ridere
questo lor ridere
ma so che in piangere
dee terminar,
dee terminar,
dee terminar!

RECITATIVO

DON ALFONSO

Si può sapere un poco la cagion di quel
riso?

GUGLIELMO

Oh cospettaccio, non vi pare che ab-
biam giusta ragione, il mio caro
padrone?

FERRANDO

Quanto pagar volete, e a monte è la
scommessa?

GUGLIELMO

Pagate la metà.

FERRANDO

Pagate solo venti quattro zecchini.

And before you forego us—
We want you to know us—
Two models of manhood!
And then these mustaches,
So rightly notorious,
What could be more glorious
A symbol of love?
                (*the women leave*)
They make us victorious
And peerless in love!
                (*laughing*)
What glorious, victorious mustaches!

SCENE XII

No. 16. TERZET

DON ALFONSO
What is so funny?

FERRANDO, GUGLIELMO
(*trying to suppress their laughter*)
We won your money!

DON ALFONSO
You are conceited!

FERRANDO, GUGLIELMO
You are defeated!

DON ALFONSO
Can't you be quiet?

FERRANDO, GUGLIELMO
You can't deny it!

DON ALFONSO
Will you be quiet, quiet, quiet, quiet!

FERRANDO, GUGLIELMO
You can't deny it, you can't deny it!

DON ALFONSO
How inconsiderate!
Why not cooperate,
Try to be patient another day.

FERRANDO, GUGLIELMO
This is hilarious!

DON ALFONSO
It's too precarious!

FERRANDO, GUGLIELMO
I can't be serious!

DON ALFONSO
You are delirious!

FERRANDO, GUGLIELMO
Ha, ha, ha, ha, ha, ha.
What a comedy,
What a display!

DON ALFONSO
There'll be a tragedy,
Sorry to say.
Control yourself,
Don't be so gay!

FERRANDO, GUGLIELMO
It is ridiculous!

DON ALFONSO
You're too meticulous!

FERRANDO, GUGLIELMO
This is too much for me,
Past my capacity,
Of all the laughs I had
This is the best.

DON ALFONSO
Laugh in your innocence,
Happy in ignorance,
But he who laughs last
Still laughs the best.

RECITATIVE

DON ALFONSO
May I ask in all politeness, what's so
    terribly funny?

GUGLIELMO
How can you ask us? I should think
    we have more than ample reason,
    most reverend benefactor.

FERRANDO
(*jokingly*)
Pay us each fifty sov'reigns and admit
    that you are beaten!

GUGLIELMO
Or pay us at least one half!

FERRANDO
I'll even settle for a mere twenty
    sov'reigns.

DON ALFONSO

Poveri innocentini! venite quà, vi
voglio porre il ditino in bocca.

GUGLIELMO

E avete ancora coraggio di fiatar?

DON ALFONSO

Avanti sera ci parlerem.

FERRANDO

Quando volete.

DON ALFONSO

Intanto silenzio e ubbidienza fino a
doman mattina.

GUGLIELMO

Siamo soldati, e amiam la disciplina.

DON ALFONSO

Or bene: andate un poco ad attend-
ermi entrambi in giardinetto, colà vi
manderò gli ordini miei.

GUGLIELMO

Ed oggi non si mangia?

FERRANDO

Cosa serve: a battaglia finita fia la cena
per noi più saporita.

No. 17. ARIA

FERRANDO

Un' aura amorosa
del nostro tesoro
un dolce ristoro
al cor porgerà.

Al cor che nudrito
da speme d'amore,
d'un esca migliore
bisogna non ha.

SCENA XIII

RECITATIVO

DON ALFONSO

Oh la saria da ridere: sì poche son le
donne costante in questo mondo e

quì vene son due! non sarà nulla —
vieni, vieni, fanciulla, e dimmi un
poco dove sono e che fan le tue
padrone?

DESPINA

Le povere buffone stanno nel giardinetto a lagnarsi coll' aria e colle
mosche d'aver perso gli amanti.

DON ALFONSO

E come credi che l'affar finirà? vogliam
sperare che faranno giudizio?

DESPINA

Io lo farei; e dove · piangon esse io
riderei, disperarsi, strozzarsi perchè
parte un amante: guardate che paz-
zia. Se ne pigliano due, s'uno va via.

DON ALFONSO

Brava! questa è prudenza. (Bisogna
impuntigliarla.)

DESPINA

E legge di natura, e non prudenza sola:
amor cos' è? piacer, comodo, gusto,
gioja, divertimento, passatempo, allegria: non è più amore se incomodo
diventa, se invece di piacer nuoce e
tormenta.

DON ALFONSO

Ma intanto queste pazze.

DESPINA

Quelle pazze? faranno a modo nostro.
E buon che sappiano d'esser amate
da color.

DON ALFONSO

Lo sanno.

DESPINA

Dunque riameranno. Diglielo si suol
dire e lascia fare il diavolo.

DON ALFONSO

E come far vuoi perchè ritornino or
che partiti sono, e che li sentano e
tentare si lasciano queste tue bestio-
line?

DON ALFONSO

Poor, inexperienced children. Just wait a bit and I will make you eat your words!

GUGLIELMO

You want to tell us you still will not give up?

DON ALFONSO

Tomorrow morning we'll talk again.

FERRANDO

I'll be delighted.

DON ALFONSO

But meanwhile, our bet is still valid up to tomorrow morning.

GUGLIELMO

We are soldiers and gave our word of honor.

DON ALFONSO

All right! I'll go ahead then and await you behind the little garden, and there you shall receive my further orders.

GUGLIELMO

And what about our dinner?

FERRANDO

What's the diff'rence? once the battle is over, it will taste that much better to the winner!

No. 17. ARIA

FERRANDO

My love is a flower,
All fragrant before me,
To soothe and restore me
With wonderful art.
Its charm and its power,
So sweet and alluring
And always enduring,
Will grow in my heart.

A spirit I nourish
With tender devotion
Forever will flourish
In glory apart.

(exeunt Ferrando and Guglielmo)

SCENE XIII

RECITATIVE

DON ALFONSO

That would be too ridiculous! I've never found a woman who's faith-

ful in this world and now I should find two! That is impossible.

(enter Despina)

There you are, my Despina. Your precious ladies, where are they? Are we making any progress?

DESPINA

Those simple-minded creatures, they're in the little garden and are telling the birds and bees of the loss of their lovers.

DON ALFONSO

What's your opinion on just how this will end? What can we do to achieve our objective?

DESPINA

Don't you worry! The more they will lament, the more I'll cheer them. All this ranting and raving for their former two lovers—I call that downright foolish. For each man who is gone, two more are waiting.

DON ALFONSO

Splendid! You are a wizzard! (It never hurts to flatter.)

DESPINA

It doesn't take much wisdom, its female intuition. For what is love? It's fun, pleasantry, gaiety, laughter, entertainment, merely pastime or a whim: once it gets serious, it is no longer love, because it is a burden and a nuisance.

DON ALFONSO

Let's think about our ladies.

DESPINA

That is simple. They'll do what we tell them. But do they realize how much they mean to our friends?

DON ALFONSO

They do.

DESPINA

Then let's prepare the groundwork. Expose them to temptation and leave the rest to nature.

DON ALFONSO

And tell me, your two indignant mistresses, now that they are so angry, how will you manage to calm them sufficiently, make them reconsider?

DESPINA

A me lasciate la briga di condur tutta
la macchina. Quando Despina macchina uno cosa, non può mancar
d'effetto: ho già menati mill' uomini
pel naso, saprò menar due femmine.
Son ricchi i due monsieurs mustacchi?

DON ALFONSO

Son richissimi.

DESPINA

Dove son?

DON ALFONSO

Sulla strada attendendomi stanno.

DESPINA

Ite, e sul fatto per la picciola porta a
me riconduceteli: v'aspetto, nella
camera mia. Purchè tutto facciate
quel ch'io v'ordinerò pria di domani
i vostri amici canteran vittoria; ed
essi avranno il gusto ed io la gloria.

SCENA XIV

No. 18. FINALE

FIORDILIGI, DORABELLA

Ah! che tutta in un momento
si cangiò la sorte mia,
ah, che un mar pien di tormento,
è la vita omai per me.

Finchè meco il caro bene
mi lasciar le ingrate stelle,
non sapea cos' eran pene,
non sapea languir cos' è.

SCENA XV

FERRANDO, GUGLIELMO

Si mora, sì, si mora,
onde appagar le ingrate.

DON ALFONSO

C'è una speranza ancora,
non fate, oh dei, non fate!

FIORDILIGI, DORABELLA

Stelle, che grida orribili!

FERRANDO, GUGLIELMO

Lasciatemi!

DON ALFONSO

Aspettate!

FERRANDO, GUGLIELMO

L'arsenico mi liberi
di tanta crudeltà.

FIORDILIGI, DORABELLA

Stelle, un velen fu quello?

DON ALFONSO

Veleno buono e bello,
che ad essi in pochi istanti
la vita toglierà.

FIORDILIGI, DORABELLA

Il tragico spettacolo
gelare il cor mi fa!

FERRANDO, GUGLIELMO

Barbare, avvicinatevi:
d'un disperato affetto
mirate il tristo effetto
e abbiate almen pietà.

FIORDILIGI, DORABELLA, FERRANDO
DON ALFONSO, GUGLIELMO

Ah! che del sole il raggio
fosco per me diventa.
Tremo, le fibre e l'anima
par che mancar si senta,
nè può la lingua o il labbro
accenti articolar.

DON ALFONSO

Giacchè a morir vicini
sono quei meschinelli
pietade almeno a quelli
cercate di mostrar.

FIORDILIGI, DORABELLA

Gente, accorrete, gente!
Nessuno, o dio, ci sente!
Despina! Despina!

DESPINA

Leave it to me. In such matters, there is no one who can equal me. When Despina manages a romance, she does not miss a chance. I have succeeded in fooling a thousand men— I can fool two women. You said your friends are very wealthy?

DON ALFONSO

Lots of money!

DESPINA

Where are they?

DON ALFONSO

They are waiting to receive further orders.

DESPINA

Splendid! Then I ask you to lead them to my room through the little garden door. I'll be ready. And I know my course of action. If both of them are willing to follow my advice, then by tomorrow your two friends will lap milk and honey, and you will win your wager, and I your money.

(*exeunt. Curtain*)

SCENE XIV

(*A flower garden. Two grassy seats on either side. Fiordiligi and Dorabella*)

No. 18. FINALIE

FIORDILIGI, DORABELLA

Ah, how sad and unrelenting
Is the fate that I must suffer,
Endless grief, cruelly tormenting,
Makes my life too hard to bear.
All was happiness and gladness
Till the moment we were parted.
Not a thought of grief or sadness,
Not a trouble, not a care,
Life was sweet and life was fair, ah—
Now the lovely dream is ended
And my joy destroyed forever.
All alone and unbefriended,
I shall die of dark despair.

SCENE XV

FERRANDO, GUGLIELMO
(*backstage*)

A double dose of poison,
That is the one solution!

DON ALFONSO

I beg you reconsider
So grim a resolution.

FIORDILIGI, DORABELLA

Heavens, that noise is horrible!

FERRANDO, GUGLIELMO

Don't hinder me!

DON ALFONSO

Not so hasty!
(*Ferrando and Guglielmo enter, each carrying a little flask, followed by Don Alfonso.*)

FERRANDO, GUGLIELMO

With arsenic upon our lips
We leave the world behind.
(*They drink, then throw their flasks to the ground; turning, they see the two women.*)

FIORDILIGI, DORABELLA

Goodness, they've taken poison?

DON ALFONSO

The strongest kind of poison,
Some arsenic and henbane
And strychnine all combined.

FIORDILIGI, DORABELLA

O tragic, woeful spectacle,
It makes my blood run cold!

FERRANDO, GUGLIELMO

Heartless, unfeeling womankind,
Our will to live is undermined.
You have disdained our wooing,
Brought on our sad undoing,
We cannot be consoled!

FIORDILIGI, DORABELLA

I'm terrified by suicide,
It frightens me to death!

ALL FIVE

All I can see is blackness,
Horror has stunned my feeling!
Trembling and shaking and shivering,
Giddy and faint and reeling,
I cannot utter a whisper,
I cannot draw a breath.
(*Ferrando and Guglielmo fall down on the grass.*)

DON ALFONSO

Frozen in rigor mortis
See how their muscles tighten!
Their handsome faces whiten
Upon the brink of death.

FIORDILIGI, DORABELLA

Help us, somebody come and help us!
We're powerless to save them!
Despina, Despina!

DESPINA
Chi mi chiama?

FIORDILIGI, DORABELLA
Despina! Despina!

DESPINA
Cosa vedo!
morti i meschini io credo,
o prossimi a spirar.

DON ALFONSO
Ah che pur troppo è vero:
furenti, disperati
si sono avvelenati,
oh amore singolar!

DESPINA
Abbandonar i miseri
saria per voi vergogna,
soccorrerli bisogna.

FIORDILIGI, DORABELLA, DON ALFONSO
Cosa possiam mai far?

DESPINA
Soccorrerli bisogna.

FIORDILIGI, DORABELLA, DON ALFONSO
Cosa possiam mai far?

DESPINA
Di vita ancor dan segno,
colle pietose mani
fate un po lor sostegno.
E voi con me correte:
un medico un antidoto
voliamo a ricercar.

FIORDILIGI, DORABELLA
Dei! che cimento è questo!
Evento più funesto
non si potea trovar!

FERRANDO, GUGLIELMO
Più bella comediola
non si potea trovar!

FERRANDO, GUGLIELMO
Ah!

FIORDILIGI, DORABELLA
Sospiran gl'infelici!

FIORDILIGI
Che facciamo?

DORABELLA
Tu che dici?

FIORDILIGI
In momenti si dolenti
chi potria li abbandonar?

DORABELLA
Che figure interessanti!

FIORDILIGI
Possiam farci un poco avanti.

DORABELLA
Ha fredissima la testa.

FIORDILIGI
Fredda, fredda è ancora questa

DORABELLA
Ed il polso?

FIORDILIGI
Io non gliel' sento.

DORABELLA
Questo batte lento, lento.

FIORDILIGI, DORABELLA
Ah se tarda ancor l'aita,
speme più non v'è di vita.

FERRANDO, GUGLIELMO
Più domestiche e trattabili
sono entrambe diventate:

FIORDILIGI, DORABELLA
Poverini, poverini!
la lor morte
mi farebbe lagrimar.

FERRANDO, GUGLIELMO
Sta a veder
che lor pietade
va in amore a terminar.

DESPINA
(backstage)
Did you call me?

FIORDILIGI, DORABELLA
Despina, Despina!

DESPINA
(entering)
What has happened?
How did they come to lie here
In such a helpless state?

DON ALFONSO
Driven by hopeless passion,
Despondent and melancholic,
They swallowed pure carbolic!
All help might come too late.

DESPINA
How can you see them lying there,
With no attention paid them?
We all must try to aid them.

FIORDILIGI, DORABELLA, DON ALFONSO
Tell us what you suggest!

DESPINA
We all must try to aid them!

FIORDILIGI, DORABELLA, DON ALFONSO
Tell us what you suggest!

DESPINA
There still are signs of life left.
Raise their heads just slightly,
Stroke their foreheads lightly,
(to Don Alfonso)
Let's run and get a doctor.
I know of one who's marvelous
With people who are ill.
He's nkown for working miracles
Without a knife or pill.
He's famous for his skill.
Perhaps he'll save them still.
(Exeunt Despina and Don Alfonso.)

FIORDILIGI, DORABELLA
What can we do, I wonder?
We made a fatal blunder
And brought about their death!

FERRANDO, GUGLIELMO
(aside)
This is so very funny,
I'll laugh myself to death!
(aloud)
Ah!

FIORDILIGI, DORABELLA
Poor fellows, they are sighing!

FIORDILIGI
(standing at quite a distance from the
two lovers)
Are they suff'ring?

DORABELLA
What do you think?

FIORDILIGI
Hear them moaning,
Loudly groaning!
Who could disregard such pain?

DORABELLA
(coming a little closer)
They have quite distinguished faces.

FIORDILIGI
(coming a little closer)
Let's advance a few more paces.

DORABELLA
This one's head is simply rigid.

FIORDILIGI
This one's arms are very rigid.

DORABELLA
Is he breathing?

FIORDILIGI
He is, but rarely.

DORABELLA
This one's pulse is beating barely.

FIORDILIGI
Help must come this very minute!

FIORDILIGI, DORABELLA
Their endurance reached the limit!

FERRANDO, GUGLIELMO
(softly)
They have lost their proud relentless-
ness,
Getting tamer by the minute.

FIORDILIGI, DORABELLA
O so helpless, so pathetic!
If they die now,
I am sure that I will cry.

FERRANDO, GUGLIELMO
I'm afraid that they may weaken,
That's a thought I can't deny,
A dreadful thought I can't deny.
(Enter Despina, disguised as a doctor.)

SCENA XVI

DON ALFONSO

Eccovi il medico,
signore belle.

FERRANDO, GUGLIELMO

Despina in maschera, che trista pelle!

DESPINA

Salvete amabiles
bones puelles.

FIORDILIGI, DORABELLA

Parla un linguaggio che non sappiamo.

DESPINA

Come comandano dunque parliamo,
So il greco e l'arabo, so il turco e il
        vandalo,
lo svevo e il tartaro so ancor parlar.

DON ALFONSO

Tanti linguaggi per se conservi:
quei miserabili per ora osservi:
Preso hanno il tossico; che si può far?

FIORDILIGI, DORABELLA

Signor Dottore, che si può far?

DESPINA

Saper bisognami
pria la cagione,
E quinci l'indole
della pozione,
se calda, o frigida,
se poca, o molta,
se in una volta,
ovvero in più.

FIORDILIGI, DORABELLA, DON ALFONSO

Preso han l'arsenico,
Signor Dottore,
Qui dentro il bebbero.
La causa è amore
Ed in un sorso
sel mandar giù.

DESPINA

Non vi affannate,
non vi turbate,
Ecco una prova
di mia virtù.

FIORDILIGI, DORABELLA, DON ALFONSO

Egli ha di un ferro
la man fornita.

DESPINA

Questo è quel pezzo
di calamita
pietra Mesmerica,
ch' ebbe l'origine
nell' Alemagna,
che poi sì celebre
là in Francia fù.

FIORDILIGI, DORABELLA, DON ALFONSO

Come si muovono,
torcono, scuotono,
in terra il cranio
presto percuotono.

DESPINA

Ah lor la fronte
tenete sù.

FIORDILIGI, DORABELLA

Eccoci pronte.

DESPINA

Tenete forte,
coraggio!
or liberi
siete da morte.

FIORDILIGI, DORABELLA, DON ALFONSO

Attorno guardano:
forze riprendono.
ah questo medico vale un Perù.

FERRANDO, GUGLIELMO

Dove son!
che loco è questo?
Chi è colui? color chi sono?
son di Giove innanzi al trono?
Sei tu Palla, o Citerea?
No, tu sei l'alma mia dea;
ti ravviso al dolce viso:
e alla man ch'or ben conosco
e che sola è il mio tesor.

DESPINA, DON ALFONSO

Son effetti ancor del tosco.
Non abbiate alcun timor.

SCENE XVI

DON ALFONSO

May I present to you Doctor Fatalis?

FERRANDO, GUGLIELMO
(to themselves)

That is Despina, just as we have planned it!

DESPINA

Salve ad libitum cum grano salis.

FIORDILIGI, DORABELLA

That may be so, but we don't understand it.

DESPINA

If you insist on it, I will translate it,
But the vernacular
Sounds less spectacular,
Completely flavorless, not recherché

DON ALFONSO

Who cares for flavor? Do us a favor,
Make a suggestion.
These frantic gentlemen have taken poison,
They swallowed arsenic
What do you say?

FIORDILIGI, DORABELLA

What are their chances?
What do you say?

DESPINA
(Feels their pulses and puts her hand to their foreheads.)

That will necessitate
Knowing the hist'ry,
I must investigate,
Study this myst'ry.
For instance, this suicide,
What caused it? The potion,
Have you a notion
If it was brown?

FIORDILIGI, DORABELLA, DON ALFONSO

They both took arsenic,
A double potion.
Love caused their suicide.
They had a bottle and with a swallow
They gulped it down.

DESPINA

I am delighted!
Don't get excited!
I'll make them well again,
As good as new.
Just let me show you
What I can do.

FIORDILIGI, DORABELLA, DON ALFONSO

He is producing a giant magnet!

DESPINA
(Touches the foreheads of the two imaginary invalids with the magnet, then gently strokes the whole length of their bodies.)

Old Doctor Besmer
Was my professor
Over in Germany.
Using his principles
Based on magnetics,
I now will demonstrate
My art to you.

FIORDILIGI, DORABELLA, DON ALFONSO

See them gesticulate,
Oscillate, palpitate,
And their convulsions are really desperate!

DESPINA

Help me support them.
They are still weak.

FIORDILIGI, DORABELLA
(putting their hands to the foreheads of the two lovers)

We'll do it gladly.

DESPINA

You're doing nicely.
That's it precisely!
They soon will be fully recovered.

FIORDILIGI, DORABELLA, DON ALFONSO

See them revive again
Fully alive again,
Thanks to the doctor's amazing technique!

FERRANDO, GUGLIELMO
(slowly raising themselves)

Am I dead? Or am I dreaming?
Is this Eden or Valhalla?
Or the garden realm of Allah?
Are you Venus?
Or Cleopatra?
No, you are my dear beloved!
Even death can't come between us.
Here's the hand I love so dearly
And would kiss with all respect.
(They embrace the women tenderly and kiss their hands.)

DESPINA, DON ALFONSO

It they talk a little queerly,
It's the magnet's strong effect.

FIORDILIGI, DORABELLA

Sarà ver, ma tante smorfie
fanno torto al nostro onor.

FERRANDO, GUGLIELMO

(Dalla voglia ch' ho di ridere,
  il polmon mi scoppia oror.)
Per pietà, bell' idol mio!
volgi a me le luci liete!

FIORDILIGI, DORABELLA

Più resister non poss' io!

DESPINA, DON ALFONSO

In porch' ore lo vedrete
per virtù del magnetismo
finire quel parossismo,
torneranno al primo umor.

FERRANDO, GUGLIELMO

Dammi un bacio, o mio tesoro,
Un sol bacio, o qui mi moro!

FIORDILIGI, DORABELLA

Stelle, un bacio?

DESPINA, DON ALFONSO

Secondate
per effetto di bontate.

FIORDILIGI, DORABELLA

Ah, che troppo si richiede
da una fida onesta amante
oltraggiata è la mia fede,
oltraggiato è questo cor.

DESPINA, FERRANDO, DON ALFONSO,
GUGLIELMO

Un quadretto più giocondo
non si vide in tutto il mondo,
quel che più mi fa da ridere
è quell' ira e quel furor.

FIORDILIGI, DORABELLA

Disperati, attossicati,
ite al diavol quanti siete;
tardi in ver vi pentirete
se più cresce il mio furor.

FERRANDO, GUGLIELMO

Dammi un bacio,
o mio tesoro,
un sol bacio,
o qui mi moro!

FIORDILIGI, DORABELLA

Disperati,
attossicati
ite al diavol
quanto siete
tardi inver
vi pentirete
se più cresce
il mio furor.

FERRANDO, GUGLIELMO

Un sol bacio!

FIORDILIGI, DORABELLA

Stelle, un bacio?

DESPINA, DON ALFONSO

Ch'io ben so che tanto foco
cangerassi in quel' d'amor.

FERRANDO, GUGLIELMO

Ne vorrei che tanto foco
terminassi in quel' d'amor.

ATTO SECONDO

SCENA I

RECITATIVO

DESPINA

Andate là, che siete due bizarre
  ragazze!

FIORDILIGI

Oh cospettaccio! cosa pretenderesti?

DESPINA

Per me nulla.

FIORDILIGI

Per chi dunque?

FIORDILIGI, DORABELLA

That may be, but such effusions
Mar the honor of my name.
Make them see that these delusions
Are a scandal and a shame.

DESPINA, DON ALFONSO

Please forgive them for their effusions,
Their condition is to blame.

FERRANDO, GUGLIELMO
(*softly*)

Though it's really too ridiculous,
I enjoy it just the same.
(*aloud*)
Take my heart and my devotion!
Do not spurn my burning ardor!

FIORDILIGI, DORABELLA

Who could hear without emotion?

DESPINA, DON ALFONSO

We are certain they'll recover.
Only wait a little longer,
Till they feel a trifle stronger.
It is too much to expect.

FERRANDO, GUGLIELMO

Kiss me, darling, I implore you,
Or I'll die right here before you!

FIORDILIGI, DORABELLA

Kiss you? Good Heavens!

DESPINA, DON ALFONSO

Better do it out of kindness!
Nothing to it.

FIORDILIGI, DORABELLA

What a shameless imposition
On good faith and true devotion,
Forcing us to give permission
For an outrage we abhor!

DESPINA, DON ALFONSO, FERRANDO,
GUGLIELMO

Since the dawning of creation
Was there ever a like flirtation?
This has been the gayest comedy
(frolic)
I have ever seen before.

FIORDILIGI, DORABELLA

Go away, you wicked madmen,
With your kisses and embraces!
Shameless, evil-minded badmen,
Never dare to show your faces
     anymore!
There is the door!

FERRANDO, GUGLIELMO

Kiss me, darling, I implore you,
Or I'll die right here before you!

FIORDILIGI, DORABELLA

Go away, you wicked madmen,
With your kisses and embraces,
We don't want to see your faces
For a single minute more!

FERRANDO, GUGLIELMO

Darling, kiss me!

FIORDILIGI, DORABELLA

Never! How dare you!

DESPINA, DON ALFONSO

Better do it
Out of kindness.
Nothing to it.

FIORDILIGI, DORABELLA

Ah, how dare you stand and face us,
After such a bold proposal?
Are you trying to disgrace us?
Never dare to show your face!
Don't come back here any more!
Do not make our anger greater,
We disdain and spurn your love!

DESPINA, DON ALFONSO

I'm convinced that soon or later
Their disdain will turn to love.

FERRANDO, GUGLIELMO

I'm afraid that soon or later
Their disdain may turn to love.

(*Curtain*)

ACT TWO

SCENE I

(*A room in the sister's home. Fiordiligi,
Dorabella, and Despina.*)

DESPINA

For Heaven's sake, how can you be
so unrealistic?

FIORDILIGI

You little devil! What is it you want?

DESPINA

Nothing for me.

FIORDILIGI

For whom then?

DESPINA

Per voi.

DORABELLA

Per noi?

DESPINA

Per voi. Siete voi donne, o no?

FIORDILIGI

E per questo?

DESPINA

E per questo dovete far da donne.

DORABELLA

Cio è?

DESPINA

Trattar l'amore en bagatelle. Le occasioni belle non negliger giammai! cangiar a tempo, a tempo esser costanti, coquettizar con grazia, prevenir la disgrazia sì comune a chi si fida in uomo, mangiar il fico, e non gittare il pomo.

FIORDILIGI

(Che diavolo!) tai cose falle tu, se n'hai voglia.

DESPINA

Io già faccio. Ma vorrei che anche voi per gloria del bel sesso faceste un po' lo stesso; per esempio: i vostri Ganimedi son andati alla guerra; infin che tornano fate alla militare: reclutate.

DORABELLA

Il cielo ce ne guardi.

DESPINA

Eh! che noi siamo in terra, e non in cielo! Fidatevi al mio zelo. Giacchè questi forestieri v'adorano lasciatevi adorar. Son ricchi, belli, nobili, generosi come fede fece a voi Don Alfonso; avean corraggio di morire per voi; questi son merti che sprezzar non si denno da giovani qual voi belle e galanti, che pon star senza amor, non senza amanti. (Par che ci trovin gusto!)

FIORDILIGI

Per Bacco ci faresti far delle belle cose; credi tu che vogliamo favola diventar degli oziosi? ai nostri cari sposi credi tu che vogliam dar tal tormento?

DESPINA

E chi dice, che abbiate a far loro alcun torto?

DORABELLA

Non ti pare, che sia torto bastante, se noto si facesse, che trattiamo costor?

DESPINA

Anche per questo c'è un mezzo sicurissimo, io voglio sparger fama, che vengono da me.

DORABELLA

Chi vuol che il creda?

DESPINA

Oh bella! non ha forse merto una cameriera d'aver due cicisbei? di me fidatevi.

FIORDILIGI

No, no, son troppo audaci questi tuoi forestieri, non ebber la baldanza fin di chieder dei baci.

DESPINA

(Che disgrazia!) io posso assicurarvi che le cose che han fatto furo effetti del tossico, che han preso, convulsioni, deliri, follie, vaneggiamenti; ma or vedrete, come son discreti, manierosi, modesti, e mansueti, lasciateli venir.

DORABELLA

E poi?

DESPINA

E poi: caspita! fate voi. (L'ho detto che cadrebbero.)

FIORDILIGI

Cosa dobbiamo far?

DESPINA

Quel che volete. Siete d'ossa, e di carne, o cosa siete?

DESPINA

For you.

DORABELLA

For us?

DESPINA

That's right. Are you both women or not?

FIORDILIGI

Can you doubt it?

DESPINA

Yes, I doubt it; you act like little schoolgirls.

DORABELLA

How so?

DESPINA

Because you think that love is serious. You must be ready when opportunity knocks. You must be equal to every new occasion, be frank or coquettish, all depending upon the man in question. That way you're always winner, and have your bread buttered on both sides.

FIORDILIGI

(What deviltry!) You may do things like that, if you want to.

DESPINA

I've always done them. But I wish that you both, for the sake of all womanhood, would follow my example. Let me tell you, now that your two Romeos have become valiant warriors, do as they did, seek your own adventures, and do it quickly.

DORABELLA

May Heaven preserve me!

DESPINA

Eh, be glad we are not yet in Heaven, but very much on earth. You have met two nice young suitors. They worship you! Then why not let them do so? They're wealthy, handsome, generous, well bred. Don Alfonso told you everything about them. They had the courage to die for your sake —is that not proof that they mean what they're saying? And aren't you both young, lovable women who deserve to be loved and adored? (Seems I am making headway!)

FIORDILIGI

I am inclined to think you want to lead us into mischief. Are you really proposing that we become the topic for gossip? And what about our lovers—do you think we would ever betray them?

DESPINA

And who said that you should. Where would be the betrayal?

DORABELLA

In my opinion, it would be bad enough if anybody heard that we met other men.

DESPINA

That is no problem. Let me take care of that for you. I'll simply spread a rumor they came to visit me.

DORABELLA

Who would believe it?

DESPINA

Why not? Any average ladies-maid has a lover—why couldn't I have two? Don't let that worry you!

FIORDILIGI

No, no! I could not do it? Those two men are so reckless! They even had the daring to beg us for kisses.

DESPINA

(Isn't that awful!) I give you my assurance that your suitors' behavior was due to the influence of poison —all their tantrums, their ravings, their fits, and all their antics. Get to know them as they really are. They are modest and decent, very polished. You'll see it for yourselves.

DORABELLA

And then?

DESPINA

And then: ask yourself! That's your business! (I knew that I could handle them.)

FIORDILIGI

What do you suggest?

DESPINA

Follow your heart. Are you made of flesh and blood, or just what are you?

No. 19. ARIA

DESPINA

Una donna
a quindici anni
dee saper
ogni gran moda,
dove il diavolo
ha la coda
cosa è beneme nal cos'è,
dee saper
la maliziette,
che innamorano
gli amanti,
finger riso,
finger pianti,
inventar i bei perché.

Dee in un momento
dar retta a cento,
colle pupille
parlar con mille,
dar speme a tutti,
sien belli o brutti,
saper nascondersi,
senza confondersi,
senza arrossire
saper mentire,
e qual regina
dall' alto soglio
col posso e voglio
farsi ubbidir.

Par ch' abbian gusto
di tal dottrina,
viva Despina
che sa servir,
che sa servir,
che sa servir!

SCENA II

RECITATIVO

FIORDILIGI

Sorella, cosa dici?

DORABELLA

Io son stordita dallo spirto infernal di
    tal ragazza.

FIORDILIGI

Ma credimi è una pazza. Ti par che
    siamo in caso di seguir suoi consigli?

DORABELLA

Oh certo se tu pigli pel rovescio il
    negozio.

FIORDILIGI

Anzi io lo piglio per il suo vero dritto:
    non credi tu delitto per due giovani
    omai promesse spose il far di queste
    cose?

DORABELLA

Ella non dice che facciamo alcun mal.

FIORDILIGI

E mal che basta il far parlar di noi.

DORABELLA

Quando si dice che vengon per
    Despina!

FIORDILIGI

Oh, tu sei troppo larga di coscienza!
    e che diranno gli sposi nostri?

DORABELLA

Nulla: o non sapran l'affare ed è tutto
    finito: o sapran qualche cosa e allor
    diremo che vennero per lei.

FIORDILIGI

Ma i nostri cori?

DORABELLA

Restano quel che sono; per divertirsi
    un poco, e non morire della malin-
    conia non si manca di fè, sorella
    mia.

FIORDILIGI

Questo è ver.

DORABELLA

Dunque?

FIORDILIGI

Dunque fa un po tu: ma non voglio
    aver colpa, se poi nasce un imbro-
    glio.

No. 19. Aria

DESPINA

Any girl fifteen or over
Must pursue a woman's mission,
And with feminine intuition
Be an expert managing men.
She must know a thousand ruses
To attract the man she chooses.
Laugh or chatter,
Weep or flatter,
Know the moment where and when.
When to amuse them,
When to confuse them,
When she should tease them,
When she should please them.
She must act slyly,
Clever and wily,
In all the ritual,
New or habitual,
Never revealing
Her inner feeling.

Love is her kingdom
She rules in splendor.
Men must surrender,
Serve her and bow.
Life can be keener,
Love can be greener,
Come to Despina,
She'll tell you how!
She'll answer questions,
Give you suggestions,
How you can handle
Gossip or scandal.
She can direct you,
She can perfect you
In all formalities
And technicalities,
Never revealing
Her inner feeling.
Love is the kingdom
She rules in splendor.
Men must surrender,
Serve her and bow!

(*exit Despina*)

SCENE II

Recitative

FIORDILIGI

I never heard such nonsense!

DORABELLA

I am speechless at the girl's unbelievable badness!

FIORDILIGI

Her theories are sheerest madness! For self-respecting women they are quite out of question!

DORABELLA

Not quite so out of question if we treat it as a joke.

FIORDILIGI

In my opinion, such a joke could be dangerous. Or do you think it proper for two ladies engaged to be married to harbor such ideas?

DORABELLA

But she assured us we'd be doing no harm.

FIORDILIGI

If people gossip, that would be harm enough.

DORABELLA

But she has offered to claim them as her suitors!

FIORDILIGI

My, what a nice, convenient type of conscience! Think of our lovers! What would they say?

DORABELLA

Nothing! Either they will not know it—in that case it is simple. Or if by chance they should hear it, then we will tell them they are Despina's friends.

FIORDILIGI

And our engagements?

DORABELLA

They will remain unbroken. An innocent diversion to pass away the tedious time of waiting can't be called a breech of faith—don't you think so?

FIORDILIGI

That is true.

DORABELLA

Well then?

FIORDILIGI

Do as you please. But remember I warned you, if something should go wrong.

DORABELLA

Che imbroglio nascer deve con tanta
precauzion, per altro ascolta, per in-
tenderci bene, qual vuoi scieglier per
te de' due Narcisi.

FIORDILIGI

Decidi tu, sorella.

DORABELLA

Io già decisi.

No. 20. Duetto

DORABELLA

Prenderò quel brunettino,
che più lepido mi par.

FIORDILIGI

Ed intanto io col biondino
vo un po ridere e burlar.

DORABELLA

Scherzosetta ai dolci detti
io di quel risponderò.

FIORDILIGI

Sospirando i sospiretti
io dell' altro imiterò.

DORABELLA

Mi dirá, ben mio, mi moro.

FIORDILIGI

Mi dirá, mio bel tesoro!

DORABELLA

Ed intanto che diletto,

FIORDILIGI

Ed intanto che diletto,

FIORDILIGI, DORABELLA

Che spassetto io proverò!

SCENA III

RECITATIVO

DON ALFONSO

Ah, correte al giardino le mie care
ragazze! che allegria! che musica!
che canto, che brillante spettacolo!
che incanto! Fate presto, correte!

DORABELLA

Che diamine esser può?

DON ALFONSO

Tosto vedrete.

SCENA IV

No. 21. Duetto con Coro

FERRANDO, GUGLIELMO

Secondate, aurette amiche,
Secondate i miei desiri,
E portate i miei sospiri
Alla dea di questo cor.

Voi, che udiste mille volte
Il tenor delle mie pene;
Ripetete al caro bene,
tutto quel che udiste allor.

CORO

Secondate, aurette amiche,
il desir di sì bei cor,
il desir di sì bei cor.

RECITATIVO

DON ALFONSO

Il tutto deponete sopra quei tavolini,
e nella barca ritiratevi, amici.

FIORDILIGI, DORABELLA

Cos' è tal mascherata?

DESPINA

Animo, via, coraggio: avete perso l'uso
della favella?

FERRANDO

Io tremo, e palpito dalla testa alle
piante.

GUGLIELMO

Amor lega le membra a vero amante.

DON ALFONSO

Da brave incorraggiateli.

DORABELLA

And what could possibly happen if we do not go too far? Just one more thing: let me ask you one question. Which of them is your choice for your admirer?

FIORDILIGI

No, you decide, dear sister.

DORABELLA

I have decided!

No. 20.   DUET

DORABELLA

I will choose the handsome dark one
If it's all the same to you.

FIORDILIGI

I myself prefer the blond one.
He is gay and winning too!

DORABELLA

I'll delight in his lovelorn phrases
With a most engaging smile.

FIORDILIGI

If he sighs and moons and gazes,
I will echo him in style.

DORABELLA

Mine will say, "My soul is burning!"

FIORDILIGI

Mine will say, "My heart is yearning!"

FIORDILIGI, DORABELLA

How romantic, how enchanting!
How amusing it will be! Ah!

DORABELLA

Mine will say, "I love you only!"

FIORDILIGI

Mine will say, "My heart is lonely!"

BOTH

How romantic, how enchanting!
It may be a little naughty,
But at least it will be fun,
A lot of fun!
(They start to leave, and run into Don Alfonso.)

SCENE III

RECITATIVE

DON ALFONSO

Ah, I'm glad that I found you! You must come into the garden! Such a frolic, with music and singing! You'll enjoy it enormously. Don't miss it! It is simply delightful!

DORABELLA

I can hardly wait to see!

DON ALFONSO

Then come with me!
(Exeunt. Curtain.)

SCENE IV

(A garden at the seashore, with grass seats and two little stone tables. A boat decorated with flowers, and a band of musicians. Servants in elaborate costumes. Despina, Ferrando, and Guglielmo on-stage. Then Don Alfonso, Fiordiligi, and Dorabella.)

No. 21.   DUET AND CHORUS

FERRANDO, GUGLIELMO

Friendly breezes, bear my message
To the one I love so dearly!
Ask her favor, beg her to hear me,
Lovely goddess that I adore!
Go and tell her, friendly breezes,
How my lonely heart is breaking,
Ever longing, ever aching!
Say I love her more and more!

CHORUS

(During this chorus, Ferrando and Guglielmo, decked with chains of flowers, rise. Don Alfonso and Despina lead them to the two women, who look at them astonished and speechless.)
Friendly breezes, bear their message
To the dear ones they adore.

RECITATIVE

DON ALFONSO

(To the servants who are bringing vases with flowers.)
Just leave all the flowers over there on the tables, and then go back to your boat, my good friends.

FIORDILIGI, DORABELLA

Why all the decorations?

DESPINA

(to Guglielmo and Ferrando)
Here is your chance, Don't miss it! Can't you speak up—or has the cat got your tongue?

FERRANDO

I'm willing, but somehow I'm a victim of stage-fright.

GUGLIELMO

It seems I have forgotten all my lines.

DON ALFONSO

Dear ladies, please encourage them.

FIORDILIGI

Parlate!

DORABELLA

Liberi dite pur quel che bramate!

FERRANDO

Madama . . .

GUGLIELMO

Anzi madame . . .

FERRANDO

Parla pur tu.

GUGLIELMO

No. no, parla pur tu.

DON ALFONSO

Oh! cospetto del diavolo! lasciate tali
smorfie del secolo passato: Despinetta, terminiam questa festa, fa tu
con lei, quel ch'io farò con questa.

No. 22. QUARTETTO

DON ALFONSO

La mano a me date,
movetevi un pò!
Se voi non parlate,
per voi parlerò.
Perdono vi chiede
un schiavo tremante,
v'offese, lo vede,
ma solo un istante;
or pena, ma tace . . .

FERRANDO, GUGLIELMO

Tace . . .

DON ALFONSO

Or lasciavi in pace . . .

FERRANDO, GUGLIELMO

In pace . . .

DON ALFONSO

Non può quel che vuole,
vorrà. quel che può.

FERRANDO, GUGLIELMO

Non può quel che vuole,
vorrà quel che può.

DON ALFONSO

Su! via! rispondete!
guardate, e ridete?

DESPINA

Per voi la risposta
a loro darò,
per voi la risposta
a loro darò.

Quello ch'è stato, è stato,
scordiamci del passato.
Rompasi omai quel laccio,
segno di servitù;
A me porgete il braccìo:
nè sospirate più.

DESPINA, DON ALFONSO

Per carità partiamo,
quel che san far veggiamo,
le stimo più
del diavolo,
s'ora non cascan giù,
le stimo più
del diavolo,
s'ora non cascan giù!

SCENA V

RECITATIVO

FIORDILIGI

Oh che bella giornata!

FERRANDO

Caldetta anzi che no.

DORABELLA

Che vezzosi arboscelli!

GUGLIELMO

Certo, certo: son belli: han più foglie
che frutti.

FIORDILIGI

Quei viali come sono leggiadri; volete
passeggiar?

FERRANDO

Son pronto, o cara, ad ogni vostro
cenno.

FIORDILIGI

Troppa grazia!

FERRANDO

(Eccoci alla gran crisi.)

FIORDILIGI
(to the lovers)

We're list'ning!

DORABELLA

Don't be afraid to say what's on your mind!

FERRANDO

My lady—

GUGLIELMO

Say "Fairest ladies."

FERRANDO

You make the speech.

GUGLIELMO

No, you, you're so much better!

DON ALFONSO

Why, this is too ridiculous! The way you are behaving is hopelessly old-fashioned. Despinetta, if they can't talk themselves, I'll do it for them. You do it for the ladies.

No. 22. QUARTET

DON ALFONSO
(Takes Dorabella by the hand.)

Step forward a little and do as I do.
(Despina takes Fiordiligi's hand.)
If you are too timid,
I will speak for you.
"If we have displeased you,
We truly lament it.
If we have disturbed you,
We deeply repent it.
Two slaves who adore you"

FERRANDO, GUGLIELMO

—dore you,

DON ALFONSO

"Have come to implore you"

FERRANDO, GUGLIELMO

Implore you,

DON ALFONSO

"Whatever you ask us, we gladly will do."

FERRANDO, GUGLIELMO
(in one big breath)

Whatever you ask us, we gladly will do.

DON ALFONSO

And now you must answer, my ladies! You are silent? You are laughing?

DESPINA
(Stands in front of the two women.)

Since they are so bashful,
So modest and shy,
I'll venture to give you my ladies' reply.
"Let us forget what happened
And think about the future.
(Despina takes Dorabella's hand, Don Alfonso Fordiligi's; the two ladies break the flower-chain around the two lovers.)
All former ties are broken.
Now we shall be good friends.
Let's join our hands in token
That all your suff'ring ends."

DESPINA, DON ALFONSO
(aside)

And now that we have spoken,
Let's watch it from a distance.
I think the ice is broken.
They need no more assistance.
I'm absolutely positive
The battle has been won,
Completely won!
The comedy is on!
(Exeunt Despina and Don Alfonso. Guglielmo are in arm with Dorabella. Ferrando and Fiordiligi more distant to each other. A short pantomimed scene, in which the four look at each other, sigh, giggle in embarrassment.)

SCENE V

RECITATIVE

FIORDILIGI

What a beautiful morning!

FERRANDO

I think it's a trifle too warm.

DORABELLA

Oh, what beautiful flowers!

GUGLIELMO

That's what I say. However they could smell a little stronger.

FIORDILIGI

In the garden there are nice shady alleys. Do you wish to promenade?

FERRANDO

With greatest pleasure! It's good for your health.

FIORDILIGI

I agree with you.

FERRANDO
(passing by Guglielmo)

(Now we are at the crossroads.)

DORABELLA

Cosa gli avete detto?

FERRANDO

Eh gli raccomandai di divertirla bene.

DORABELLA

Passeggiamo anche noi.

GUGLIELMO

Come vi piace. Ahimè!

DORABELLA

Che cosa avete?

GUGLIELMO

Io mi sento sì male, sì male, anima mia, che mi par di morire.

DORABELLA

(Non otterà nientissimo.) Saranno i rimasugli del velen che beveste.

GUGLIELMO

Ah che un veleno assai più forte io bevo in que' crudi e focosi mongibelli amorosi!

DORABELLA

Sarà veleno calido; fatevi un poco fresco.

GUGLIELMO

Ingrata, voi burlate, ed intanto io mi moro! (Son spariti: dove diamin son iti?)

DORABELLA

Eh via non fate.

GUGLIELMO

Io mi moro, crudele, e voi burlate?

DORABELLA

Io burlo? io burlo?

GUGLIELMO

Dunque datemi qualche segno, anima bella, della vostra pietà.

DORABELLA

Due, se volete; dite quel che far deggio, e lo vedrete.

GUGLIELMO

(Scherza, o dice davvero?) Questa picciola offerta d'accettare degnatevi.

DORABELLA

Un core?

GUGLIELMO

Un core: è simbolo di quello ch'arde, languisce e spasima per voi.

DORABELLA

(Che dono prezioso!)

GUGLIELMO

L'accettate?

DORABELLA

Crudele, di sedur non tentate un cor fedele.

GUGLIELMO

(La montagna vacilla: mi spiace ma impegnato è l'onor di soldato.) V'adoro!

DORABELLA

Per pietà!

GUGLIELMO

Son tutto vostro!

DORABELLA

Oh Dei!

GUGLIELMO

Cedete, o cara!

DORABELLA

Mi farete morir.

GUGLIELMO

Morremo insieme, amorosa mia speme. L'accettate?

DORABELLA

L'accetto.

GUGLIELMO

(Infelice Ferrando!) Oh che diletto!

No. 23. DUETTO

GUGLIELMO

Il core vi dono,
bell' idolo mio;
ma il vostro vo' anch'io,
via datelo a me.

FIORDILIGI

What was it that you told him?

FERRANDO

Oh, I was only saying there's moss on the road.

DORABELLA

Shall we too take a walk?

GUGLIELMO

I am all for it!
      (*They walk.*)
Good Lord!

DORABELLA

Is something wrong?

GUGLIELMO

All at once I feel dreadful—perhaps it's some kind of fever—I may even be dying.

DORABELLA

(I don't believe a word of it.) You still are feeling effects from the poison you've taken.

GUGLIELMO

There is a far more deadly poison, a far more fatal danger, in the flame of your two glorious eyes.
(*Fiordiligi strolls off with Ferrando.*)

DORABELLA

A flattering comparison! You ought to write a poem!

GUGLIELMO

You really should not tease me, when you know how I'm suff'ring. (I can't see them. Are they hiding on purpose?)

DORABELLA

Don't be so silly!

GUGLIELMO

You are heartless and cruel to go on joking!

DORABELLA

I'm joking? You think so?

GUGLIELMO

Won't you show me a sign of pity, fairest of ladies, to uphold my morale?

DORABELLA

Only too gladly. Merely say what you wish and you shall have it!

GUGLIELMO

(She's fooling, or could she have meant it?) Will you do me one favor. Let me give you this locket.

DORABELLA

A heart?

GUGLIELMO

Yes, darling! A most appropriate symbol to reassure you of my everlasting love.

DORABELLA

(Oh, dear, it is charming!)

GUGLIELMO

You accept it?

DORABELLA

I'd like to, but my heart is not free, as you well know.

GUGLIELMO

(The iceberg is melting. I'm sorry, but my soldierly word can't be broken.) I love you!

DORABELLA

Please don't!

GUGLIELMO

I love you madly!

DORABELLA

Don't say it!

GUGLIELMO

Do not reject me!

DORABELLA

I insist that you go!

GUGLIELMO

If you reject me I'm determined to perish! You'll accept it?

DORABELLA

(*after a short hesitation, with a sigh*
I will then!

GUGLIELMO

(What a blow for Ferrando!) I am delirious!

No. 23.   DUET

GUGLIELMO

This heart is for you, dear,
My only beloved!
Give me yours to treasure
As long as I live!

DORABELLA

Mel date, lo prendo,
ma il mio non vi rendo,
invan me'l chiedete,
più meco ei non è.

GUGLIELMO

Se teco non l'hai,
perchè batte quì?

DORABELLA

Se a me tu lo dai,
che mai balza lì?

GUGLIELMO

Perchè batte, batte, batte qui?

DORABELLA

Che mai balza, balza, balza lì?

DORABELLA, GUGLIELMO

Perchè batte, batte, batte quì?
È il mio coricino,
che più non è meco,
ei venne a star teco,
ei batte così.

GUGLIELMO

Quì lascia ch' il metta.

DORABELLA

Ei quì non può star.

GUGLIELMO

T'intendo furbetta,
t'intendo furbetta.

DORABELLA

Che fai?

GUGLIELMO

Non guardar.

DORABELLA

Nel petto un Vesuvio
d'avere mi par.

GUGLIELMO

(Ferrando meschino!
possibil non par.)

GUGLIELMO

L'occhietta a me gira.

DORABELLA

Che brami?

GUGLIELMO

Rimira, rimira,
se meglio può andar.

DORABELLA, GUGLIELMO

Oh cambio felice,
di cori e d'affetti!
che nuovi diletti,
che dolce penar!

SCENA VI

RECITATIVO

FERRANDO

Barbara! perchè fuggi?

FIORDILIGI

Ho visto un aspide, un' idra, un basilisco!

FERRANDO

Ah! crudel, ti capisco! L'aspide, l'idra,
il basilisco, e quanto i Libici deserti
han di più fiero, in me solo tu vedi.

FIORDILIGI

E vero, è vero. Tu vuoi tormi la pace.

FERRANDO

Ma per farti felice.

FIORDILIGI

Cessa di molestarmi!

FERRANDO

No ti chiedo ch'un guardo.

FIORDILIGI

Partiti!

FERRANDO

Non sperarlo, se pria gli occhi men fieri
a me non giri! O ciel! ma tu mi
guardi e poi sospiri?

DORABELLA

I take it with pleasure,
But one thing I'll tell you:
The heart that you ask for
Is not there to give.

GUGLIELMO

Whose heart do I hear then,
If your heart is gone?

DORABELLA

Whose heart is so near then,
If I have your own?

GUGLIELMO

What is beating, beating loud and
clear?

DORABELLA

What is throbbing, throbbing in my
ear?

BOTH

What is beating, beating loud and
clear?
It must be my own heart,
My loving and lone heart,
A heart which is yours now
For ever and ever!
A heart true as gold,
To have and to hold!

GUGLIELMO

(*Wants to put the heart where she
keeps the portrait of her lover.*)
And now you must wear it!

DORABELLA

I really don't dare.

GUGLIELMO

You rascal, I know you!
Just wait till I show you!

DORABELLA

What is it?
(*He gently turns her face the other way,
then takes away the portrait and puts
the heart in its place.*)
Don't look yet.

DORABELLA
(*to herself*)

I feel so excited,
Aglow and on fire,
So strangely delighted
And filled with desire.

GUGLIELMO
(*to himself*)

Ferrando, poor fellow!
His future looks dire.

(*aloud*)

And now you may see it.

DORABELLA

Oh, may I?

GUGLIELMO

Look here, dear,
Now what do you say?

BOTH

How joyful a union
Of hearts and affection,
The noblest perfection
That love can attain!
How joyful a union
Of thought and of feeling,
So sweetly revealing
The wonder of love!

(*They leave, arm in arm.*)

SCENE VI
(*Enter Ferrando and Fiordiligi.*)

RECITATIVE

FERRANDO

You torture me! Why do you leave me?

FIORDILIGI

I've seen monstrosities, a hydra, a
writhing serpent!

FERRANDO

Now I grasp the allusion! All of them,
the hydra, the writhing serpent, and
all the horrifying monsters you could
imagine you have seen in my person.

FIORDILIGI

It's true, I admit it. You have caused
me such anguish.

FERRANDO

For your happiness only.

FIORDILIGI

If you would only leave me!

FERRANDO

All I ask is one glance.

FIORDILIGI

Never!

FERRANDO

You dismiss me, abandon me to grief
and desperation! Dear God! Is there
no hope, no consolation?

No. 24. ARIA

FERRANDO

Ah! io veggio quell' anima bella
al mio pianto resister non sà:
non è fatta per esser rubella
agli affetti di amica pietà.
In quel guardo, in quei cari sospiri,
dolce raggio lampeggia al mio cor:
già rispondi a miei caldi desiri,
già tu cedi al più tenero amor.

Ma tu fuggi,
spietata tu taci,
ed invano mi senti languir?
Ah, cessate speranze fallaci,
la crudel mi condanna a morir.

SCENA VII

RECITATIVO

FIORDILIGI

Ei parte ... senti ... Ah no! partir si
lasci, si tolga ai sguardi miei l'infausto oggetto della mia debolezza.
A qual cimento il barbaro mi pose!
un premio è questo ben dovuto a
mie colpe! In tale istante dovea di
nuovo amante, i sospiri ascoltar?
l'altrui querele dovea volger in
gioco? Ah, questo core a ragione
condanni, o giusto amore! Io ardo
e l'ardor mio non è più effetto d'un
amor virtuoso: è smania, affanno,
rimorso, pentimento, leggerezza, per-
fidia, è tradimento!

No. 25. RONDO

FIORDILIGI

Per pietà, ben mio, perdona
all' error d'un alma amante
fra quest' ombre, e queste piante
sempre ascoso, oh Dio, sarà!

Svenerà quest' empia voglia

l'ardir mio, la mia costanza,
perderà la rimembranza,
che vergogna e orror mi fà.

A chi mai mancò di fede
questo vano ingrato cor?
si dovea miglior mercede,
caro bene, al tuo candor,
caro bene, al tuo candor.

SCENA VIII

RECITATIVO

FERRANDO

Amico, abbiamo vinto!

GUGLIELMO

Un ambo, o un terno?

FERRANDO

Una cinquina, amico;
Fiordiligi è la modesta in carne.

GUGLIELMO

Niente meno?

FERRANDO

Nientissimo; sta atteno e ascolta come
fù.

GUGLIELMO

T'ascolto; di pur sù.

FERRANDO

Pel giardinetto come eravam d'accor-
do, a passeggiar mi metto; le do il
braccio; si parla di mille cose in-
differenti; alfine viensi all'amor.

GUGLIELMO

Avanti.

FERRANDO

Fingo labbra tremanti,
fingo di pianger, fingo di morir al
suo piè.

GUGLIELMO

Brava assai per mia fè! Ed ella?

FERRANDO

Ella da prima ride, scherza, mi burla—

No. 24. ARIA

FERRANDO

(*happily*)

Though you try to be deaf to my
    pleading,
I am sure you will yield in the end.
You're not meant to be cold and
    unheeding
To the love of so faithful a friend.
All your glances, so demure and
    appealing,
Make my heart glow with soft, radiant
    light.
You will yield to the force of my
    feeling,
To its boundless endurance and might.
You'll surrender to its endless delight!
But you spurn me, disdainful, uncaring,
Coldly leave me to languish and sigh!
Ah, I'm hopeless, abandoned,
    despairing,
For you cruelly condemn me to die!
(*Exit.*)

SCENE VII

RECITATIVE

FIORDILIGI

I hurt him! Should I . . . ? ah, no!
It's better this way. At least I
will not see him, the wretched person who has caused me to weaken.
What grievous anguish the cruel man
has brought me! But I deserve it
for my shameless behavior! At such
a moment how could I ever listen to
a new lover's plea? Should I have
treated his proposal more lightly?
Yes, I am guilty. I am punished quite
justly. O dear Guglielmo! This stran-
ger, he has aroused my heart to
passion, not to love, true and perfect.
This passion is restless, disturbing,
and deceitful, superficial! It's wicked,
faithless betrayal!

No. 25. RONDO

FIORDILIGI

Dearest love, I beg your pardon
For the faith that I have broken.
May my error remain unspoken,
Stay forgotten, unknown and past.
May my honest, true devotion,

Glowing love, and deep repentance
Purge my heart of all remembrance,
Make me worthy of you at last.

Why did I embrace temptation,
Break the tender vows I swore,
When it was my aspiration
To be faithful evermore?

Heaven grant me one kind favor,
Let my secret remain unknown.
With unfailing endeavor
For my fault I shall atone.
(*exit*)

SCENE VIII

(*enter Ferrando and Guglielmo*)

RECITATIVE

FERRANDO

(*deliriously happy*)

Guglielmo, it can't go better!

GUGLIELMO

I knew it, I knew it!

FERRANDO

Yes, you have your wager. Fiordiligi
is the rock of Gibraltar!

GUGLIELMO

Nothing less?

FERRANDO

No, nothing! Now listen: I'll tell you
how it went.

GUGLIELMO

I'm listening. Go ahead.

FERRANDO

As we agreed, both of us went strolling
together in the garden, arm in arm,
just chatting. At first we talked about
the weather and then we talked
about love.

GUGLIELMO

Go on, friend.

FERRANDO

I said all I could hink of, swore that
I loved her, threatened to die at
her feet.

GUGLIELMO

My dear boy, you did well! And she?

FERRANDO

At the beginning she was laughing and
joking.

GUGLIELMO

E poi?

FERRANDO

E poi finge d'impieto sirsi—

GUGLIELMO

Oh cospettaccio!

FERRANDO

Alfin scoppia la bomba: "pura come
colomba al suo caro Guglielmo ella
si serba" mi discaccia superba, mi
maltratta, mi fugge, testimonio ren-
dendomi e messaggio, che una femmina ell' è senza paraggio.

GUGLIELMO

Bravo tu! bravo io! brava la mia
Penelope! lascia un po ch'io ti ab-
bracci per sì felice augurio, o mio
fido Mercurio!

FERRANDO

E la mia Dorabella? come s'è dipor-
tata? Oh non ci ho neppur dubbio!
assai conosco quella sensibil alma.

GUGLIELMO

Eppur un dubbio, parlando di quattr'
occhi, non saria mal, se tu l'avessi!

FERRANDO

Come?

GUGLIELMO

Dico così per dir! (avrei piacere
d'indorargli la pillola.)

FERRANDO

Stelle! cesse ella forse alle lusinghe tue?
ah, s'io potessi sospettarlo soltanto!

GUGLIELMO

E sempre bene il sospettare un poco
in questo mondo.

FERRANDO

Eterni Dei! favella: a foco lento non
mi far quì morir; ma no, tu vuoi
prenderti meco spasso: ella non ama,
non adora che me.

GUGLIELMO

Certo! anzi in prova di suo amor, di
sua fede questo bel ritrattino ella
mi diede.

FERRANDO

Il mio ritrato! Ah perfida!

GUGLIELMO

Ove vai?

FERRANDO

A trarle il cor dal scellerato petto,
e a vendicar il mio tradito affetto.

GUGLIELMO

Fermati!

FERRANDO

No, mi lascia!

GUGLIELMO

Sei tu pazzo? vuoi tu precipitarti per
una donna, che non val due soldi?
(Non vorrei, che facesse qualche cor-
belleria!)

FERRANDO

Numi! tante promesse e lagrime, e
sospiri, e giuramenti in sì pocchi
momenti come l'empia obliò!

GUGLIELMO

Per Bacco io non lo so!

FERRANDO

Che fare or deggio! a qual partito, a
qual idea mi appiglio? Abbi di me
pietà, dammi consiglio!

GUGLIELMO

Amico, non saprei qual consiglia a te
dar!

FERRANDO

Barbara! ingrata! in un giorno! in
poch'ore!

GUGLIELMO

Certo un caso quest'è da far stupore.

GUGLIELMO

And then?

FERRANDO

For a moment I thought she wavered.

GUGLIELMO

That little vixen!

FERRANDO

But then, bang! went the bombshell. "Dare you question my virtue? I will always be faithful to my Guglielmo." She began to abuse me, called me names, and left me. So you see from her attitude there's no doubt. Fiordiligi is one woman in a million.

GUGLIELMO

Good for you, good for me, good for my faithful sweetheart! You're a friend in a million, bringer of happy tidings. I'm deliriously happy!

(they embrace)

FERRANDO

And my dear Dorabella? How did you fare with her? Why do I even ask you!

(enthusiastically)

I know your answer! How could I even doubt it?

GUGLIELMO

A little doubting, my dear undoubting Thomas, might be advisable at times.

FERRANDO

How so?

GUGLIELMO

O, it was just a thought. (I wish I knew how to sweeten his cup of bitterness!)

FERRANDO

Braggart! Are you implying she yielded to your advances? No, it can't be! I will never suspect her!

GUGLIELMO

You would be wiser to leave a little room for some suspicion.

FERRANDO

What do you mean? Speak up! If you must poison me, must it be drop by drop? But no. It can't be! Tell me that you are joking! I am her love and she loves only me.

GUGLIELMO

Surely! And to prove the fact beyond any question, she gave me this delightful little portrait.

FERRANDO

(raging)

Gave you my portrait! Ah, shame on her.

(starts to leave)

GUGLIELMO

Are you raving?

FERRANDO

(furiously)

No, I am not, but she will pay me dearly for her misdeed. How could she dare betray me?

GUGLIELMO

Calm yourself!

FERRANDO

(determined)

No, I cannot!

GUGLIELMO

This is madness! Why do you want to wreck yourself for a women so completely worthless? (If I could just prevent his from doing something foolish.)

FERRANDO

Think of it! Her deep devotion, her promises, her affection and protestations — all forgotten entirely in the wink of an eye!

GUGLIELMO

That seems to be the case.

FERRANDO

My life is ruined! What shall I do now? What use is there in living? I'm in a dreadful state! Help me, I beg you!

GUGLIELMO

I wish I could advise you, but I really don't know.
Horrible! My future! All in shambles! Torn assunder!

GUGLIELMO

This is really a case that makes you wonder!

No. 26. ARIA

GUGLIELMO

Donne mie, la fate a tanti! a
tanti, a tanti, a tanti, a tanti!
che, se il ver vi deggio dir,
se si lagnano gli amanti,
li commincio a compatir.
Io vo bene al sesso vostro,
lo sapete, ognun lo sà,
ogni giorno ve lo mostro,
vi do segno d'amistà.

Ma quel farla a tanti e tanti, a
tanti e tanti,
m'avvilisce in verità.
Mille volte il brando presi,
per salvar il vostro onor,
mille volte, mille volte,
mille volte vi difesi
colla bocca, e più col cor.

Ma quel farla a tanti e tanti, a
tanti e tanti,
à eun vizietto seccator.
Siete vaghe, siete amabili,
più tesori il ciel vi diè;
e le grazie vi circondano,
dalla testa sino ai pié.
Ma, ma, ma la fate a tanti e tanti, a
tanti e tanti,
che credibile non è.

Ma la fate a tanti e tanti,
a tanti e tanti, a tanti,
la fate a tanti e tanti, a tanti e tanti,
che se gridano gli amanti,
hanno certo un gran perchè.

SCENA IX

RECITATIVO

FERRANDO

In qual fiero contrasto, in qual dis-
ordine di pensieri e di affetti io mi
ritrovo? Tanto insolito e novo è il
caso mio, che non altri, non io basto
per consigliarmi . . . Alfonso! Alfonso! quanto rider vorrai della mia
stupidezza! Ma, mi vendicherò! saprò

dal seno cancellar quell' iniqua . . .
saprò cancellarla—cancellarla? Troppo, o Dio, questo cor per lei mi parla.

No. 27. CAVATINA

FERRANDO

Tradito, schernito,
dal perfido cor,
io sento,
che ancora
quest' alma
l'adora.
Io sento
per essa
le voci
d'amor.

RECITATIVO

DON ALFONSO

Bravo! questa è costanza.

FERRANDO

Andate, o barbaro, per voi misero sono.

DON ALFONSO

Via se sarete buono vi tornerò l'antica
calma. Udite: Fiordiligi a Guglielmo
si conserva fedel, e Dorabella infedel
a voi fù.

FERRANDO

Per mia vergogna.

GUGLIELMO

Caro amico, bisogna far delle differenze in ogni cosa. Ti pare che una
sposa mancar possa a un Guglielmo?
un picciol calcolo, non parlo per
lodarmi; se facciamo tra noi . . . tu
vedi, amico, che un poco di può
merto.

DON ALFONSO

Eh anch'io lo dico!

GUGLIELMO

Intanto mi darete cinquanta zecchin-
etti.

No. 26. ARIA

GUGLIELMO

I would like a word with all you lovely,
Lovely, lovely women.
I have something on my mind.
It's a basic human problem
And it touches all mankind.
Like my fellowmen and brothers,
I have worshipped before your shrine.
Like a million others,
I believed you were divine.
I've respected
And protected
Your good name in ev'ry way,
Yes, in each and ev'ry way.
But, you thankless, lovely, lovely,
    lovely women
Fill my soul with deep dismay.
With my sword I saved your virtue,
I have fought a fearless fight.
I've discovered
And uncovered
Ev'ry plot designed to hurt you.
I have been your peerless knight.
But, you wicked, lovely, lovely, lovely
    women
Put my chivalry to flight.
You're delightful, you're adorable,
You are precious, you are sweet,
You are gracious, fair, and lovable,
And we men are at your feet.
But, but, but,
You thankless, lovely, lovely, lovely
    women
Shock my heart with your deceit.
In the most poetic phrases
I have sung your sex's praises,
I have lauded
And applauded
And extolled you to the sky.
But, but, but, you wicked, lovely
    women,
When I see how you mistreat us
I begin to wonder why.
                (exit)

SCENE IX

RECITATIVE

FERRANDO

I can scarcely imagine that I myself
have become the prey of a woman's
ruthless deception! I'm so stunned
by misfortune, so disillusioned, I
feel helpless, defeated, totally dazed
and hopeless! Alfonso, Alfonso! You
were right after all! Now you will be
triumphant! But I shall be avenged!
I'll tear her image from my heart
and my mem'ry, and shall not regret
her! Not regret her? No, dear God,
I cannot! I can't forget her!

No. 27. CAVATINA

FERRANDO

Defeated, mistreated,
Despairing, forlorn!
I'll never forget her,
I'll always adore her
And ever regret her,
The love that I mourn.
Rejected, neglected,
My heart grieved and sore!
(*Don Alfonso enters with Guglielmo.
They stay in the background, listen-
ing to Ferrando.*)
I still love her dearly,
Forever sincerely.
My love is as great
And as strong as before.
(*Don Alfonso and Guglielmo step for-
ward.*)

RECITATIVE

DON ALFONSO

Bravo. That's how it should be.

FERRANDO

Stay away from me! You have caused
all my misery!

DON ALFONSO

Learn how to bear it calmly, and you
will be so much the wiser. The fact
is, Fiordiligi was faithful, at least up
to now, but Dorabella was too weak
to resist.

FERRANDO

Yes, to my shame.

GUGLIELMO

Dear Ferrando, you must be able to
see a thing in its true aspect. Where
would you find a woman who would
fail a Guglielmo? If you compare us
—I say it in all modesty—you will
have to admit, if you are honest, I
have a slight advantage.

DON ALFONSO

He's got a point there.

GUGLIELMO

And now, suppose you pay me half of
the wager.

DON ALFONSO

Volontieri: pria però di pagar vo che
facciamo qualche altra esperienza.

GUGLIELMO

Come?

DON ALFONSO

Abbiate pazienza: Infin domani siete
entrambi miei schiavi: a me voi deste
parola da soldati, di for quel ch'io
dirò. Venite; io spero mostrarvi ben
che folle è quel cervello, che sulla
frasca ancor vende l'uccello.

SCENA X

RECITATIVO

DESPINA

Ora vedo che siete una donna di garbo.

DORABELLA

Invan, Despina, di resister tentai: quel
demonietto ha un artifizio, un elo-
quenza, un tratto, che ti fà cader
giù se sei di sasso.

DESPINA

Corpo di satanasso, questo vuol dir
saper, tanto di raro noi povere
ragazze abbiamo un po di bene, che
bisogna pigliarlo allor ch'ei viene. Ma
ecco la sorella, che ceffo!

FIORDILIGI

Sciagurate! ecco per colpa vostra in
che stato mi trovo!

DESPINA

Cosa è nato, cara Madamigella?

DORABELLA

Hai qualche mal, sorella?

FIORDILIGI

Ho il diavolo, che porti me, te, lei,
Don Alfonso, i forestieri e quanti
passi ha il mondo.

DORABELLA

Hai perduto il giudizio?

FIORDILIGI

Peggio, peggio, inorridisci: io amo! e
l'amor mio non è sol per Guglielmo.

DESPINA

Meglio, meglio!

DORABELLA

E che si, che anche tu se' innamorata
del galante biondino?

FIORDILIGI

Ah, pur troppo per noi.

DESPINA

Ma brava!

DORABELLA

Tieni, settanta mille baci: tu il biondino, io'l brunetto, eccoi entrambe
spose!

FIORDILIGI

Cosa dici? non pensi agli infelici, che
stamane partir? ai loro pianti, alla
lor fedeltà tu più non pensi? Così
barbari sensi, dove, dove apprend-
esti? sì diversa da te come ti festi?

DORABELLA

Odimi: sei tu certa, che non muojano
in guerra i nostri vecchi amanti?
e allora? entrambe resterem colle
man piene di mosche: tra un bon
certo e un incerto c'è sempre un
gran divario.

FIORDILIGI

E se poi torneranno?

DORABELLA

Se torneran lor danno! noi saremo
allor mogli, noi saremo lontane mille
miglia.

FIORDILIGI

Ma non so, come mai si può cangiar
in un sol giorno un core.

DORABELLA

Che domanda ridicola! siam donne!
e poi tu com' hai fatto!

DON ALFONSO

I'll be glad to, but before I shall do it, permit me to try one more test.

GUGLIELMO

You mean?

DON ALFONSO

I'm not yet defeated. Until tomorrow you are bound to our wager, and just remember, you gave your word of honor to obey my command. Till then, I will not give up the ship, and I am still competing, for the proof of the pudding is in the eating!

(*exeunt. Curtain*)

SCENE X

(*A room with several doors, a mirror, and a little table. Dorabella and Despina on-stage.*)

RECITATIVE

DESPINA

Now at last you are acting like a woman of the world.

DORABELLA

I was not able to resist the temptation. That charming devil is so persuasive, he is so clever, so gentle, he would even succeed in melting millstones.

DESPINA

Now you are talking logic and really showing sense! Only too seldom are we poor girls permitted to snatch a bit of pleasure, so it is up to us to make hay while the sun shines! Who's coming? It's your sister. She's raving!

FIORDILIGI

How disgraceful! It's on account of you that I am in this dilemma.

DESPINA

What has happened? Why are you so excited?

DORABELLA

Is something wrong, dear sister?

FIORDILIGI

I hope the devil takes you all, you, -and her, Don Alfonso, those two intruders! And all the fools in this world!

DORABELLA

Are you out of your mind?

FIORDILIGI

Worse than that! Dare I admit it? I love him! And worst of all is, I do not mean Guglielmo!

DESPINA

Sounds exciting.

DORABELLA

Do you mean that you've also started yielding, and you love your new suitor?

FIORDILIGI

(*sighing*)

Ah, yes, only too much!

DESPINA

Delightful!

DORABELLA

Sister, I simply have to kiss you. Then we both will be married! What could be more romantic!

FIORDILIGI

But how can we? Just think of our poor soldiers who have gone to the wars! Have you no feeling for those two faithful men, the grief we'd cause them? How could we deceive them? What has come over you, that you want to commit such a betrayal?

DORABELLA

Wait a bit! How do we know that the worst might not happen? Suppose they fell in battle? In that case, what would become of us? Wouldn't we be the losers? You know the saying: A bird in the hand is worth two in the bush!

FIORDILIGI

But if they should return?

DORABELLA

In that event, it's their loss! By that time we'll be married, and what's more, we'll be living abroad.

FIORDILIGI

I am still at loss to understand this sudden change of heart.

DORABELLA

That is downright ridiculous! We're women! After all, what did you do?

FIORDILIGI

Io saprò vincermi.

DESPINA

Voi non saprete nulla.

FIORDILIGI

Farò, che tu lo veda.

DORABELLA

Credi sorella, è meglio che tu ceda.

No. 28. ARIA

DORABELLA

E amore un ladroncello,
un serpentello è amor,
ei toglie e dà la pace,
come gli piace ai cor.

Per gli occhi al seno appena
un varco aprir si fa,
che l'anima in catena,
e toglie libertà.

E amore un ladroncello,
un serpentello è amor,
ei toglie e dà la pace,
come gli piace ai cor.

Porta dolcezza,
dolcezza e gusto,
se tu lo lasci far,
ma t'empie di disgusto,
se tenti ti pugnar.

E amore un ladroncello,
un serpentello è amor.
ei toglie e dà la pace,
come gli piace ai cor.

Se nel tuo petto ei siede,
s'egli ti becca quì,
fa tutto quel ch'ei chiede,
che anch'io farò così.

SCENA XI

RECITATIVE

FIORDILIGI

Come tutto conguira a sedurre il mio
cor! ma no! si mora, e non si ceda!
errai quando alla suora io mi
scopersi ed alla serva mia. Esse a
lui diran tutto, ed ei più audace,
fia di tutto capace, agle occhi mai
più non comparisca! a tutti i servi
minacierò il congedo, se lo lascian
passar, veder nol voglio quel seduttor.

GUGLIELMO

(Bravissima! la mia casta Artemisia!
la sentite?)

FIORDILIGI

Ma potria Dorabella senza saputa
mia — piano! un pensiero per la
mente mi passa: in casa mia restar
molte uniformi di Guglielmo e di
Ferrando, ardir! Despina! Despina!

DESPINA

Cosa c'è!

FIORDILIGI

Tieni un po questa chiave e senza
replica, senza replica alcuna, prendi
nel guardaroba, e quì mi porta due
spade, due cappelli, e due vestiti
de' nostri sposi.

DESPINA

E che volete fare?

FIORDILIGI

Vanne, non replicare.

DESPINA

(Comanda in abregè donna Arro-
ganza.)

FIORDILIGI

Non c'è altro; ho speranza che Dorabella stessa seguirà il bell' esempio:
al campo, al campo, altra strada
non resta per serbaci innocenti.

FIORDILIGI

But I'm not surrendering!

DESPINA

There you are quite mistaken!

FIORDILIGI

I won't! I'll never do it!

DORABELLA

Come, dearest sister, you must, or you will rue it.

No. 28. ARIA

DORABELLA

I know a naughty fellow,
A wily thief called Love.
He slyly steals your calmness,
Sweet as a turtle-dove.
The moment he has found you,
He wounds you with his dart—
He ties his chains around you
And rules your helpless heart,
I know a naughty fellow,
A wily rogue called Love,
He slyly steals your calmness,
Sweet as a turtle-dove.
He can be charming, divine, delightful,
If he's allowed his way,
But also cruel and spiteful,
Malevolent and spiteful,
If you should disobey.
I know a naughty fellow,
A wily thief called Love.
He slyly steals your calmness,
Sweet as a turtle-dove.
Each time his fire brands you,
Raging inside your breast,
Do all that he commands you
And better not protest.
If he should come and seize you,
Pulling your heart-strings tight,
Just let the rascal tease you
And do not try to fight.
Just let him seize you,
And tickle and tease you!
Just let the rascal seize you and
   tease you,
As I intend to do,
I too,
As I intend to do.
   (*Despina leaves with Dorabella.*)

SCENE XI

RECITATIVE

FIORDILIGI

How they're plotting together to make me break my word! But no! I will not! I'd rather die. I never should have talked to Dorabella, or even to Despina. They might tell him my secret, and thus encouraged, I could never control him. I must avoid him, not even let him see me. I will give orders that any of my servants will be dismissed on the spot if they should dare to let him come near me.

GUGLIELMO

(*listening at the door, unseen by Fiordiligi*)

(By Jupiter! What a model of virtue! Let's hear more!)

FIORDILIGI

I'm afraid Dorabella cannot be persuaded. Wait! An idea! Now I know what to do! By some good fortune Guglielmo and Ferrando left some uniforms behind. That's lucky. Despina, Despina!

DESPINA

(*enters*)

My lady called?

FIORDILIGI

Go up to the attic, and without questioning and without contradiction, open your masters' trunks and bring me two helmets, two sabers, and two complete uniforms they left there.

DESPINA

What for, if I may ask you?

FIORDILIGI

Go, do as I told you!

DESPINA

(What a high and mighty tone! It is disgusting.)
   (*leaves*)

FIORDILIGI

I am determined. Now my problem is getting Dorabella to consent to go with me. The sooner, the better. It's the only solution to preserve our integrity.

DON ALFONSO
(Ho capito abbastanza: vanne pur non temer.)

DESPINA
Eccomi.

FIORDILIGI
Vanne: sei cavalli di posta, voli un servo ordinar, di a Dorabella che parlarle vorrei.

DESPINA
Sarà servita (Questa donna mi par di senno uscita.)

FIORDILIGI
L'abito di Ferrando sarà buono per me; può Dorabella prender quel di Guglielmo; in questi arnesi raggiungerem gli sposi nostri, a loro fianco pugnar potremo e morir se fa d'uopo: ite in malora, ornamenti fatali, io vi detesto.

GUGLIELMO
(Si può dar un amor simile a questo?)

FIORDILIGI
Di tornar non sperate alla mia fronte pria ch'io qui torni col mio ben; in vostro loco porrò questo cappello; oh come ei mi trasforma le sembianze e il viso! come appena io medesma or mi ravviso!

No. 29. Duetto

FIORDILIGI
Fra gli amplessi, in pochi istanti,
giungerò del fido sposo,
sconosciuta a lui davanti
in quest' abito verrò.

Oh che gioja il suo bel core
proverà nel ravvisarmi!

FERRANDO
Ed intanto di dolore
meschinello, io mi morrò!

FIORDILIGI
Cosa veggio!
son tradita!
Deh, partite!

FERRANDO
Ah, no mia vita:
con quel ferro di tua mano
questo cor tu ferirai,
e se forza oh Dio non hai,
io la man ti reggerò.

FIORDILIGI
Taci, ahimè! son abbastanza
tormentata ed infelice!

FERRANDO
Ah che omai la sua costanza,

FIORDILIGI
Ah, che omai la mia costanza,

FIORDILIGI, FERRANDO
A quei sguardi, a quel che dice,
Incomincia a vacillar.

FIORDILIGI
Sorgi, sorgi—

FERRANDO
Invan lo credi.

FIORDILIGI
Per pietà, da me che chiedi?

FERRANDO
Il tuo cor, o la mia morte.

FIORDILIGI
Ah non son, non son più forte!

FERRANDO
Cedi cara—

FIORDILIGI
Dei, consiglio!

FERRANDO
Volgi a me pietoso il ciglio,
in me sol trovar tu puoi
sposo, amante, e più, se vuoi,
idol mio, più non tardar.

DON ALFONSO

(*at the door to Despina, who returns*)
(I see what she's up to. Better do what she says.)

DESPINA

There you are.

FIORDILIGI

Thank you. Now order us horses and a man we can trust. Tell Dorabella that I want her at once.

DESPINA

I'm at your service. (This to-do and commotion is beyond me!)
(*Exit.*)

FIORDILIGI

This uniform of Ferrando should be just about my size, and Dorabella can wear one of Guglielmo's. Disguised as soldiers, we two can go and find our sweethearts. If it must be, we shall fight beside them. Even death shall not part us!
(*Throws off her headdress.*)
Off with this head-gear, this insane decoration. Oh, how I hate it!

GUGLIELMO

Her devotion and courage are astounding!

FIORDILIGI

Not until I return with my beloved shall it adorn my head again! And, in its stead, this helmet will disguise me! Now off to war and adventure! I'll be lucky, I'm certain! Not a soul will suspect that I'm a woman!

No. 29.   DUET

FIORDILIGI

By tomorrow we'll be united!
I will join you, dear Guglielmo!
Unexpected, your Fiordiligi
Will appear in her disguise.
What a wonderful surprise!
You'll be joyful and so delighted
When you see your faithful sweetheart!
(*stepping forward*)

FERRANDO

And I'll die here, unrequited,
Right before your very eyes!

FIORDILIGI

Why are you here? Oh, how dreadful!
Spare my feelings?

FERRANDO

Before you leave me,
(*Takes his sword from the table, and draws it from its sheath.*)
Take this sword and plunge it through me,
Through this loving heart you wounded!
Take this sword and pierce my heart!

FIORDILIGI

Never! Please go! I have endured too much unhappiness already!

FERRANDO

Her resistance starts to weaken.

FIORDILIGI

My resistance starts to weaken.

BOTH

Now my (her) courage is less steady,
And my (her) will is failing fast.

FIORDILIGI

Do not tempt me!

FERRANDO

I beg you, hear me!

FIORDILIGI

Why on earth must you pursue me?

FERRANDO

Take my life or say you love me!
(*He takes her hand and covers it with kisses.*)

FIORDILIGI

He is strong and so appealing!
I will yield, I have a feeling.

FERRANDO

Dearest angel, say you love me!
Don't resist me any longer!

FIORDILIGI

God above me!

FERRANDO

(*with great tenderness*)
Always obey your heart's true feeling,
Yield to love sincere and tender.
Dearest, I beg you, you must surrender!
Do not let me plead in vain!

FIORDILIGI

Giusto ciel!
crudel! hai vinto
Fa di me quel che ti par!

FIORDILIGI, FERRANDO

Abbracciamci, o caro bene,
e un conforto a tante pene
sia languir di dolce affetto,
di diletto sospirar.

SCENA XIII

RECITATIVO

GUGLIELMO

Oh poveretto me! cosa ho veduto!
cosa ho sentito mai!

DON ALFONSO

Per carità! silenzio!

GUGLIELMO

Mi pelerei la barba! mi graffierei la
pelle! e darei colle corna entro le
stelle, fu quella Fiordiligi? la Penelope, l'Artemisia del secolo! bric-
cona, assassina furfante, ladra, cagna!

DON ALFONSO

Lasciamolo sfogar—

FERRANDO

Ebben!

GUGLIELMO

Dov' è!

FERRANDO

Chi? la tua Fiordiligi?

GUGLIELMO

La mia Fior, Fior di diavolo, che
strozzi lei prima e dopo me!

FERRANDO

Tu vedi bene, v'han delle differenze
in ogni cosa, un poco di più merto—

GUGLIELMO

Ah cessa! cessa di tormentarmi, ed una
via piuttosto studiam di castigarle
sonoramente.

DON ALFONSO

Io so, qual è: sposarle.

GUGLIELMO

Vorrei sposar piuttosto la barca di
Caronte.

FERRANDO

La grotta di Vulcano.

GUGLIELMO

La porta dell' Inferno.

DON ALFONSO

Dunque restate celibi in eterno.

FERRANDO, GUGLIELMO

Mancheran forse donne ad uomin
come noi?

DON ALFONSO

Non c'è abbondanza d'altro. Ma l'altre,
che faran, se ciò fer queste? In fondo
voi le amate queste vostre cornacchie
spennacchiate.

FERRANDO, GUGLIELMO

Ah pur troppo! Pur troppo!

DON ALFONSO

Ebben pigliatele com' elle son, natura
non potea fare l'eccezzione, il privi-
legio, di creare due donne d'altra
pasta, per i vostri bei musi; in ogni
cosa, ci vuol filosofia. Venite meco;
di combinar le cose, studierem la
maniera vo che ancor questa sera
doppie nozze si facciano. Frattanto
un' ottava ascoltate: felicissimi voi,
se la imparate.

No. 30

DON ALFONSO

Tutti accusan le donne,
ed io le scuso,
se mille volte al dì cangiano amore,

FIORDILIGI
(*trembling*)

Gracious Lord! Gracious Lord!
I am frail! I fail!
Have pity! I have fought my love
in vain!

(*Guglielmo wants to rush in, but Don
Alfonso holds him back.*)

BOTH

I'm so happy, it's past believing!
All our tortured hours of grieving
Are forgotten now forever!
We shall never part again!
Dearest heart,
We shall never part again!

(*Exeunt Fiordiligi and Ferrando.*)

SCENE XIII

RECITATIVE

GUGLIELMO

This should happen to me! To a
Guglielmo! Victimized by a woman!

DON ALFONSO

Compose yourself, I beg you!

GUGLIELMO

The devil with composing! I'm madder
than a hornet! I feel like flying
through the ceiling! So that is Fiordiligi! Model of virtue! My rock of
Gibraltar! That vixen, that hyena,
that serpent, tigress, viper!

DON ALFONSO
(*unruffled*)

Let him get it off his mind.

FERRANDO
(*entering*)

What now?

GUGLIELMO

Where is she?

FERRANDO

Who? Your good Fiordiligi?

GUGLIELMO

My good Fior—good for nothing! The
devil may take her, and me with her.

FERRANDO

Do you remember? I say it without
the least bit of conceit, "I have a
slight advantage!"

GUGLIELMO

Keep quiet! This is no time for joking.
We'd better think of some way to
punish those two hussies most
severely.

DON ALFONSO

I'll tell you how. Marry them!

GUGLIELMO

I'd much rather marry the devil's
grandmother!

FERRANDO

And I an ugly ogress!

GUGLIELMO

Or any female dragon!

DON ALFONSO

Then you will end your days as lonely
bachelors.

FERRANDO

For men of our kind there are women
a-plenty!

DON ALFONSO

I do not deny that. However, do you
think they would be diff'rent? You
might as well admit it, you love
your unfaithful little sweethearts.

DON ALFONSO

Yes, we love them!

FERRANDO

We love them!

DON ALFONSO

Why don't you marry them just as
they are? What gives you the right
to demand of nature to make ex-
ceptions and create two super-
human women, just because you
would like it? We cannot alter what
has already happened. There's only
one way to make your future happy.
I will make the arrangements, and
before it is evening you shall both
wear a wedding ring. And now let
me tell you an adage. If you take it
to heart, it's to your advantage.

No. 30

DON ALFONSO

Women cannot be faithful,
But I don't mind it,
For I can see the principle behind it.

altri un vizio lo chiama,
ed altri un uso,
ed a me par necessità del core.
L'amante che si trova al fin deluso,
non condanni l'altrui, ma il proprio
    errore:
giacchè giovani, vecchie, e belle e
    brutte,
ripetete con me:
Così fan tutte!

FERRANDO, DON ALFONSO, GUGLIELMO
Così fan tutte.

SCENA XIV

RECITATIVO

DESPINA
Vittoria padroncini! a sposarvi dis-
poste son le care madame: a nome
vostro loro io promisi, che in tre
giorni circa partiranno con voi:
l'ordin mi diero, di trovar un notajo,
che stipuli il contratto: alla lor
camera attendendo vi stanno. Siete
così contenti?

FERRANDO, GUGLIELMO, DON ALFONSO
Contentissimi.

DESPINA
Non è mai senza effetto, quand' entra
la Despina in un progetto.

SCENA XV

No. 31. FINALE

DESPINA
Fate presto, o cari amici,
alle faci il foco date,
e la mensa preparate
con ricchezza e nobiltà!
Delle mostre padroncine
gl'imenei son pià disposti:
e voi gite ai vostri posti
finchè i sposi vengon quà.

CORO
Facciam presto, o cari amici,
Alle faci il foco diamo,
e la mensa preparate
con ricchezza e nobiltà.

DON ALFONSO
Bravi, bravi!
ottimamente!
che abbondanza, che eleganza!
una mancia conveniente
l'un el l'altro a voi darà.
Le due coppie omai si avvanzano,
fate plauso al loro arrivo,
lieto canto e suon giulivo
empia il ciel d'ilarità.

DESPINA, DON ALFONSO
La più bella comediola

SCENA XVI

CORO
Benedetti
i doppi conjugi,
e le amabili
sponsine:
splenda lor
il ciel benefico,
ed a guisa
di galline
sien di figli
ognor prolifiche
che le agguaglino
in beltà.

FIORDILIGI, DORABELLA, FERRANDO,
GUGLIELMO
Come par che qui prometta
tutto gioja e tutto amore!
Della cara Despinetta
certo il merito sarà.

Radoppiate il lieto suono,
replicate il dolce canto,
e noi qui seggiamo intanto
in maggior giovialità.

You are wrong to upbraid them.
You have to take them as they are,
As Mother Nature made them.
You lovers, don't complain of
 disillusion.
What you need is to reach the wise
 conclusion:
All your ancestors, fathers, and
 brothers went through it.
Since they learned it from Eve:
Women always betray,
That's how they do it.

ALL THREE

"Così fan tutte!"

SCENE XIV

(Enter Despina.)

RECITATIVE

DESPINA

Hurrah for our two winners! The ladies have decided to consent to the wedding, and shortly after, according to your wishes, they will be prepared to depart from the city. They gave me orders to arrange all the details. The notary is ready. So are the witnesses. You may go now to see them. Well, are you pleased and happy?

FERRANDO, GUGLIELMO, DON ALFONSO

Overwhelmingly!

DESPINA

In affairs of this kind depend upon Despina's master-mind!
 (Curtain.)

SCENE XV

(A hall, richly decorated and illuminated. An orchestra at the back. Table set for four people, with silver candlesticks. Four servants in rich costumes. Despina, the Servants and Musicians.)

No. 31. FINALE

DESPINA

Go ahead and light the candles
And complete the decorations.
Make the final preparations.
Soon the couples will be here!
We must do our ladies honor
At their wedding celebration.
         (to the musicians)
Let us plan a great ovation
When the brides and grooms appear.

SERVANTS, MUSICIANS

Go ahead and light the candles
And complete the decorations.
Make the final preparations.
Soon the couples will be here.

DON ALFONSO

(While he sings, the musicians tune their instruments.)

This is perfect! I am delighted!
This is splendid, simply splendid!
I shall see that you're commended
In a most substantial way.
When the couples make their
 entrances,
At my signal gather near them.
Wish them luck and loudly cheer them.
Clap your hands and shout hurray.

DESPINA, DON ALFONSO

I am absolutely certain
That the ev'ning will be gay!
Very soon we'll raise the curtain
On the play within the play.

(Exeunt Despina and Don Alfonso through different doors.)

SCENE XVI

(As the two sets of lovers enter, the Chorus sings and the orchestra begins a march.)

CHORUS

Heaven bless you with prosperity
And success in each endeavor.
With our heartfelt, true sincerity
May we wish you joy forever.
May you live in perfect harmony,
Carefree, peaceful, and untroubled,
And attain redoubled happiness
With your children at your side.
Hail the bridegroom and the bride!

FIORDILIGI, DORABELLA, FERRANDO,
GUGLIELMO

Fortune showers us with favor!
Life can hold no greater promise!

FIORDILDIGI, DORABELLA

Thank you, dearest Despinetta,

FERRANDO, GUGLIELMO

For our happiness tonight!

ALL FOUR

Dearest friends, continue singing
In your bright and merry chorus!
Sing to happy days before us
And a life of new delight!

(The betrothed couples eat.)

CORO

Benedetti i doppi conjugi ecc.

FERRANDO, GUGLIELMO

Tutto, tutto, o vita mia,
al mio foco, or ben risponde!

FIORDILIGI, DORABELLA

Pel mio sangue l'allegria
cresce, cresce e sì diffonde!

FERRANDO, GUGLIELMO

Sei pur bella!

FIORDILIGI, DORABELLA

Sei pur vago!

FERRANDO, GUGLIELMO

Che bei rai!

FIORDILIGI, DORABELLA

Che bella bocca!

FERRANDO, GUGLIELMO

Tocca e bevi,

FIORDILIGI, DORABELLA

Bevi e tocca,

FERRANDO, GUGLIELMO

Tocca, bevi,

FIORDILIGI, DORABELLA, FERRANDO,

Tocca, tocca, bevi, bevi, tocca!
E nel tuo, nel mio bicchiero
si sommerga ogni pensiero,
E non resti più memoria
del passato ai nostri cor.

GUGLIELMO

(Ah, bevessero del tossico,
Queste volpi senza onor.)

SCENA XVII

DON ALFONSO

Miei Signori, tutto à fatto;
col còntratto nuziale
il notajo è sulle scale
e ipso facto qui verrà.

FIORDILIGI, DORABELLA, FERRANDO,
GUGLIELMO

Bravo, bravo! passi subito.

DON ALFONSO

Vò a chiamarlo:
eccolo quà.

DESPINA

Augurandovi ogni bene,
il notajo Beccavivi
coll' usata a voi sen viene
notariale dignità!
È il contratto stipulato
colle regole ordinarie,
nelle forme giudiziarie,
pria tossendo, poi sedendo
clara voce leggerà.

FIORDILIGI, DORABELLA, FERRANDO,
GUGLIELMO

Bravo, bravo, in verità!

DESPINA

Per contratto da me fatto
si congiunge in matrimonio
Fiordiligi con Sempronio,
e con Tizio Dorabella,
sua legitima sorella,
quelle dame ferraresi,
questi nobili albanesi,
e per dote e contradote . . .

FIORDILIGI, DORABELLA, FERRANDO,
GUGLIELMO

Cose note, cose note!
vi crediamo,
ci fidiamo, soscriviam,
date pur quà!

DESPINA, DON ALFONSO

Bravi, bravi, in verità!

CORO

Bella vita militar,
ogni dì si cangia loco,
oggi molto e noman poco,
ora in terra ed or sul mar.

FIORDILIGI, DORABELLA, DESPINA,
FERRANDO, GUGLIELMO

Che rumor! che canto è questo!

DON ALFONSO

State cheti; io vò guardar.
Misericordia!
Numi del cielo!
Che caso orribile!
io tremo! io gelo!
gli sposi vostri—

FIORDILIGI, DORABELLA

Lo sposo mio!

CHORUS

Heaven bless you with prosperity, etc.

FERRANDO, GUGLIELMO

Happy, happy end of sorrow,
Bright new promise of joy hereafter!

FIORDILIGI, DORABELLA

Glowing hope for life tomorrow,
Filled with tender love and laughter!

FERRANDO, GUGLIELMO

You're my angel!

FIORDILIGI, DORABELLA

You're my hero!

FERRANDO, GUGLIELMO

Say you love me!

FIORDILIGI, DORABELLA

I'll always love you!

FERRANDO, GUGLIELMO

Here's to gladness!

FIORDILIGI, DORABELLA

Let's be happy!
Drink a toast to happy days together!
(They clink their glasses.)

FERRANDO, GUGLIELMO

Drink to happiness together!

FIORDILIGI, DORABELLA, FERRANDO

May the glow of wine's contentment
Heal our woe and drown all
　　resentment.
May our sorrow and our sadness
Swiftly vanish from our mem'ry
　　forevermore.

GUGLIELMO

Ah, just to think of their dishonesty
Makes me wish there had been poison
　　in their wine.
(enter Don Alfonso)

SCENE XVII

DON ALFONSO

Now it's time that we proceeded
With the signing of the contract.
We have ev'rything that's needed,
And the couples both are here.

BOTH COUPLES

We are ready, call the notary!

DON ALFONSO ..

Honored Counselor Illegalis,
Kindly come in.
(Enter Despina, disguised as a notary.)

DESPINA

"Cornucopia verborum,"
As we always say in Latin.
Since we have a legal quorum,
I suggest that we proceed.
Here's the bona fide agreement
With the statement of the causes
And the modifying clauses.
With decorum,
Harum, horum,
I shall now begin to read.

THE COUPLES

Very well, proceed, proceed!

DESPINA
(with a nasal tone)

Marriage is the sworn intention
Of the parties I now mention.
Fiordiligi and Sempronio,
Dorabella and Antonio,
Ladies hereby called "the sisters",
To the designated misters,
Latter nobles of Albania,
Dowry, gifts, and miscellanea . . .

THE COUPLES

Never mind it, never mind it,
We will read it when we've signed it
Later on! Hand us a pen!
(Only the two women sign the
　contract.)

DESPINA, DON ALFONSO

Happy ladies, lucky men!
(Don Alfonso takes the contract. The
　sound of drums and singing is heard.)

CHORUS
(off-stage)

On to glory, on to war!
We are free of care and sorrow,
Here today and there tomorrow
Over land and over sea!

COUPLES, DESPINA

Hear that song! It sounds familiar!

DON ALFONSO

Wait a moment, let me look!
(He goes to the window.)
O boundless misery! Heaven preserve
　us!
What a catastrophe! How awful!
　How dreadful!
Your former sweethearts!

FIORDILIGI, DORABELLA

Our former sweethearts!

DON ALFONSO

in questo istante
tornaro, o Dio, ed alla riva
sbarcano già!

FIORDILIGI, DORABELLA, FERRANDO,
GUGLIELMO

Cosa mai sento!
Barbare stelle! in tal momento,
che si farà?

FIORDILIGI, DORABELLA

Presto partite!
Presto fuggite!

DESPINA, FERRANDO, DON ALFONSO,
GUGLIELMO

Ma se li (ci) veggono?
Ma se li (ci) incontrano?

FIORDILIGI, DORABELLA

Là, là, celatevi, per carità!
Numi! soccorso!
Numi, consiglio!
Chi dal periglio ci salverà?
chi?

DON ALFONSO

Rasserenatevi,
Ritranquillatevi!
In me fidatevi,
ben tutto andrà.

FIORDILIGI, DORABELLA

Mille barbari pensieri
tormentando il cor mi vanno,
se discoprono l'inganno,
ah, di noi che mai sarà!

SCENA ULTIMA

FERRANDO, GUGLIELMO

Sani e salvi agli amplessi amorosi,
delle nostre fidissime amanti,
ritorniamo di gioja esultanti,
per dar premio alla lor fedeltà.

DON ALFONSO

Giusti Numi! Guglielmo! Ferrando!
o che giubilo! qui,
come,
e quando?

FERRANDO, GUGLIELMO

Richiamati da regio contrordine,
pieni il cor di contento e di gaudio,
ritorniamo alle spose adorabili,
ritorniamo alla vostro amistà.

GUGLIELMO

Ma cos' è quel pallor, quel silenzio?

FERRANDO

L'idol mio, perchè mesto si stà?

DON ALFONSO

Dal diletto confuse ed attonite,
Mute, mute si restano là.

FIORDILIGI, DORABELLA

Ah, che al labbro le voci mi mancano.
Se non moro, un prodigio sarà.

GUGLIELMO

Permettete che sia posto
quel baul in quella stanza.
Dei! che veggio! un uom nascosto?
un notajo? qui che fa?

DESPINA

Non Signor non è un notajo,
è Despina mascherata,
che dal ballo or è tornata,
e a spogliarsi, venne quà.

FIORDILIGI, DORABELLA

La Despina, la Despina!
Non capisco come cà.

FERRANDO, GUGLIELMO

Una furba uguale a questa.
dove mai si troverà?

DON ALFONSO

I see them landing down at the
  mooring.
I hate to say so, but it is true!

COUPLES

O this is shocking! How can we stay
  them?
At least delay them,
What can we do?
(*The servants take the table away, and
the musicians hurry off.*)

FIORDILIGI, DORABELLA
(*to Ferrando and Guglielmo*)

You cannot stay here!
Either you hide yourselves or run away!

THE OTHER FOUR

If they discover you, what will they
  do to you (us)?
(*Fiordiligi and Dorabella hide their
lovers in one room. Don Alfonso leads
Despina to another room.*)

FIORDILIGI, DORABELLA
(*frantically*)

Heaven protect us! Heaven preserve
  us!
Who will advise us in our dismay?

DON ALFONSO

Just put your trust in me!
I'll save the day!

FIORDILIGI, DORABELLA

I have never been so frightened,
So upset and so bewildered.
If they learn how we deceived them,
Heaven knows what we can say!

LAST SCENE

(*Fiordiligi and Dorabella on-stage. Ferrando and Guglielmo enter, in their
soldier uniforms and hats.*)

FERRANDO, GUGLIELMO

We are home, safe and sound from
  our journey,
Our perilous journey!
How we've longed for a glimpse of
  your faces!
How we've yearned for your tender
  embraces,
For your love so sincere to the end!

DON ALFONSO

Well, I never! Guglielmo! Ferrando!
This is marvelous!
You! Back here? So quickly!

FERRANDO, GUGLIELMO

Our commander has altered his
  strategy.
To our joy we were called back to
  Naples.
With our hearts full of wonderful
  happiness
We return to our sweethearts and
  friend.

GUGLIELMO
(*to Fiordiligi*)

Dearest love, why so pale and so silent?

FERRANDO
(*to Dorabella*)

Dearest heart, why this sorrowful air?

DON ALFONSO

They are totally speechless from
  happiness.
You took them unaware,
That should show you how deeply
  they care!

FIORDILIGI, DORABELLA
(*aside*)

I am speechless with terror and
  misery!
I am ready to die of despair!

GUGLIELMO

If you ladies will permit us,
We will put away our baggage.
What does this mean? Is someone
  hiding?
An attorney? Who is this?

DESPINA
(*Enters, without wearing her notary's
hat.*)

I am neither man nor lawyer
But Despina pure and simple.
I was trying on my costume
For tomorrow's masquerade.

FIORDILIGI, DORABELLA

How she fooled us so completely
Is a mystery to me.
It's Despina! How on earth could it
be she?

FERRANDO, GUGLIELMO

There is no one like Despina.
That is plain enough to see!
(*Don Alfonso discreetly lets the contract signed by the ladies fall to the
floor.*)

DESPINA

Una furba che m'agguagli
dove mai si troverà!

DON ALFONSO

Già cader lasciai le carte,
raccoglietele con arte.

FERRANDO

Ma che carte sono queste?

GUGLIELMO

Un contratto nuziale?

FERRANDO, GUGLIELMO

Giusto ciel! voi quì scriveste,
contradirci omai non vale,
tradimento, tradimento,
ah si faccia il scoprimento;
e a torrenti, a fiumi, a mari
indi il sangue scorrerà!

FIORDILIGI, DORABELLA

Ah! Signor son rea di morte
e la morte io sol vi chiedo,
il mio fallo tardi vedo,
con quel ferro un sen ferite
che non merita pietà!

FERRANDO, GUGLIELMO

Cosa fù?

FIORDILIGI, DORABELLA

Per noi favelli
il crudel, la seduttrice.

DON ALFONSO

Troppo vero è quel che dice,
e la prova è chiuso lì!

FIORDILIGI, DORABELLA

Dal timor io gelo, io palpito:
perchè mai li discoprì!

FERRANDO

A voi s'inchina
bella damina!
il Cavaliere dell' Albania.

GUGLIELMO

Il ritrattino
pel coricino,
ecco io le rendo
Signora mia.

FERRANDO, GUGLIELMO

Ed al magnetico
Signor Dottore
rendo l'onore
che meritò.

FIORDILIGI, DORABELLA, DESPINA

Stelle! che veggo!
Al duol non reggo!

FERRANDO, DON ALFONSO, GUGLIELMO

Son stupefatte!
Son mezze matte!

FIORDILIGI, DORABELLA

Ecco là il barbaro che c'ingannò.

DON ALFONSO

V'ingannai, ma fu l'inganno
disinganno ai vostri amanti,
che più saggi omai saranno
che faran quel ch'io vorrò.
Quà le destre, siete sposi,
abbracciatevi e tacete.
Tutti quattro ora ridete,
Ch'io già risi e riderò

DESPINA

There is no one like Despina,
There is no one else like me.

DON ALFONSO
(softly to the lovers)

Here's the evidence you needed!
Take this document and read it.

FERRANDO

May I ask what's in this paper?

GUGLIELMO

Are you willing to explain it?
Can it be a marriage contract?

FERRANDO, GUGLIELMO

What a crime! And you have signed it!
To deny your guilt is useless!
To my horror I discover
You betrayed your faithful lover!
You will not escape my vengeance!
Streams of guilty blood will flow!
(They try to go into the other room,
    but the ladies hold them back.)

FIORDILIGI, DORABELLA

Ah, I beg of you to kill me.
I am guilty, as you declare me.
Show no pity, do not spare me!
Take your saber and do your duty.
I will welcome it, for I deserve it so!

FERRANDO, GUGLIELMO

Tell the truth!

FIORDILIGI, DORABELLA

(Point to Despina and Don Alfonso.)
These are the traitors!
All we did was their suggestion.

DON ALFONSO

That is true without a question.
I can prove it very well.
(Shows them the room where the lovers
    had gone to hide. Ferrando and Gug-
    lielmo go into the room for a mo-
    ment, then come out, without the
    hats, coats, and beards, but with the
    outer clothing of their former dis-
    guise, in the comic manner they had
    formerly affected.)

FIORDILIGI, DORABELLA

What a dreadful trick to play on us!
Oh, why did he have to tell?

FERRANDO

You are my goddess! I kneel before
    you!
I am your hero who wants to adore
    you!

GUGLIELMO
(to Dorabella)

Here is a portrait I know you treasure.
Give me my heart now, measure for
    measure.

FERRANDO, GUGLIELMO
(to Despina)

Let us congratulate Doctor Fatalis,
Master of Magnets, the paragon!

FIORDILIGI, DORABELLA, DESPINA

Gracious! amazing!
Stunning and dazing!

FERRANDO, DON ALFONSO, GUGLIELMO

They're struck by thunder!
Speechless with wonder!

FIORDILIGI, DORABELLA
(pointing to Don Alfonso)

Here is the guilty one
Who led us on!

DON ALFONSO

Yes, I did, but my deception
Was to undeceive your lovers
And to prove there's no exception
To a rule that's always true.
Learn your lesson, heed the moral!
Let's be friends again! End your
    quarrel!
Laugh about what's past and over
And I'll laugh along with you.

FIORDILIGI, DORABELLA

Idol mio, se questo è vero,
colla fede e coll' amore
compensar saprò il tuo core,
adorarti ognor saprò!

FERRANDO, GUGLIELMO

Te lo credo, gioja bella,
ma la prova io far non vò.

DESPINA

Io non so se questo è sogno,
mi confondo, mi vergogno:
manco mal se a me l'han fatta,
che a molt' altri
anch'io la fò.

FIORDILIGI, DORABELLA, DESPINA
FERRANDO, DON ALFONSO, GUGLIELMO

Fortunato l'uom, che prende
ogni cosa pel buon verso,
e tra i casi, e le vicende
da ragion guidar si fà.

Quel che suole altrui far piangere
fia per lui cagion di riso,
e del mondo in mezzo i turbini,
bella calma troverà.

FIORDILIGI, DORABELLA

Dear beloved, please forgive me!
Oh, my sweetheart, I hope to show
    you
All the loving faith I owe you!
I will prove my worth to you.
(*The lovers join hand and embrace
    each other.*)

FERRANDO, GUGLIELMO

You don't have to, my beloved,
I shall ask no proof from you.

DESPINA

I who was the master schemer
Find myself a baffled dreamer.
I have learned a useful lesson,
Something that I never knew.
Tricks you play on other people,
Other people play on you!

ALL

Happy is the man of reason
Who can face the world in season.
Firm and steadfast
And uncomplaining,
He will go his cheerful way.
Things that make his brothers
    sorrowful,
He will answer with knowing laughter.
He has learned that life's adversities
Turn to joy another day.